What people are saying about …

THE SACRED SEARCH

"Singles, pay attention. Gary knows marriage and is eager to help those of us desiring marriage get there with confidence and grace."

Lisa Anderson, Focus on the Family
director of young adults and host of
The Boundless Show, www.boundless.org

"It's what drives so many industries and even more individuals: it's the pursuit of the perfect spouse. But what if there's more—*much more*—to dating than finding 'the one'? In *The Sacred Search*, my friend Gary Thomas looks at the heart of a subject that many consider him an expert on—successful marriage. And with a biblical and bold approach, he shows readers that marriage isn't just about who we walk down the aisle with but also about the very reasons behind that walk. Anyone who is dating, engaged, or hopes to be one day needs to read this book!"

Ed Young, senior pastor of Fellowship Church,
author of *New York Times* bestseller *Sexperiment*

"Gary Thomas has logged a lot of miles working with young men and women as they navigate the often difficult path to marriage in the twenty-first century. *The Sacred Search* will help those who desire marriage to pursue it in a manner that deepens their faith, honors God, and blesses their future spouses."

Jim Daly, president of Focus on the Family

"Gary Thomas debunks the mythical search for a soul mate to help you choose a 'sole mate'—someone who will 'lay down their life' in faithful love. This biblically based book is for anyone who wants to be wise in pursuit of a spouse."

Drs. Les and Leslie Parrott, authors of
Saving Your Marriage before It Starts

"You may know *Sacred Marriage*. *The Sacred Search* will ask you why you want to be married. Filled with questions to make you think and teaching that will bring 'aha' moments, this book is a must-read for everyone considering marriage. I highly recommend it to you—I wish I'd had it when I was single!"

Linda Dillow, author of bestselling
Calm My Anxious Heart and
What's It Like to Be Married to Me?

"*The Sacred Search* is a powerfully honest portrayal of the biblical view of marriage. Gary Thomas dismantles contemporary philosophies on love, sexuality, and marital union by offering strong arguments for why they have not been successful. His comprehensive look at romantic relationships through psychological, emotional, physical, and spiritual perspectives gives the reader a framework for understanding the *why* of marriage in a world that is grossly fixated on the *who*. His appeal to a kingdom-first perspective gives both hope and healing for a generation in desperate need of a fresh and Christ-centered understanding of God's plan for marriage. This book is a must-read before anyone says 'I do.'"

Dr. Michelle Anthony, family ministries
executive pastor at New Life Church
and author of *Spiritual Parenting* and
Dreaming of More for the Next Generation

"Our culture is obsessed with compatibility and chemistry. However, in relationship formation, character always trumps chemistry. Great marriages do not flow from compatibility; they flow from character. I appreciate Gary Thomas taking such a bold stand on marriage. *The Sacred Search* is a gut check for anyone considering, delaying, or even pursuing marriage. If marriage scares you, read this book and be encouraged. If you feel you are not ready for marriage, then please read and be prepared. If the critics tell you it ain't worth it, I beg you to read this book and learn how to honor marriage."

Ted Cunningham, author of
Young and in Love and *Trophy Child*

"One of the primary hopes I have for my generation is that we will desire partnerships with purpose. In this book, Gary creates a compelling argument that shifts the believer's view of relationships, dating, and marriage to focus on something greater. His biblical, logical, and fatherly wise advice is the reason I will point my generation to his book for many of the commonly asked 'What about ...' questions. And I will point the older generation to him as a guide to mentoring my peers. I'm thankful Gary has created this resource. Guess I can quit my job now!"

Joy Eggerichs, director of
Love and Respect (Now)

"Something is broken. Marriages are falling apart all around us, and I believe Gary Thomas has just gone straight to the root. We build our entire lives on this earth around this one decision (who to marry): where we live, how we live. Even future humans hang in the balance. Gary just built a map to help you see through the emotion and infatuation to God's heart for dating and marriage."

Jennie Allen, author of *Anything*

"In *The Sacred Search*, Gary Thomas clearly, relevantly, and scripturally debunks common myths that stunt singles. He helps us see the fallacy of searching for our 'soul mate' and waiting around for 'the one.' This book will help singles make wiser choices about who we marry because it explores why we marry."

Lindsey Nobles, blogger

"'Why should I get married?' could be the most important question millennials are asking. Gary Thomas helps this generation navigate the 'why' in a Christ-honoring way. A long-awaited tool for how singles can navigate the difficult waters of dating and how to make finding a mate a holy pursuit."

Esther Fleece, culture communicator, millennial expert, and former millennial relations assistant at Focus on the Family

THE
SACRED

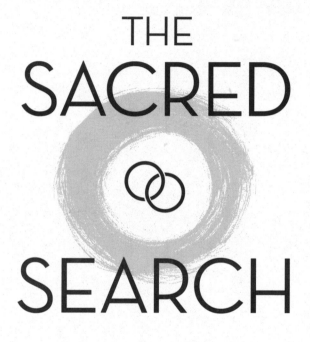

SEARCH

UPDATED & REVISED

BESTSELLING AUTHOR OF *SACRED MARRIAGE*

GARY THOMAS

THE
SACRED
SEARCH

What if It's Not about
Who You Marry, but Why?

transforming lives together

THE SACRED SEARCH
Published by David C Cook
4050 Lee Vance Drive
Colorado Springs, CO 80918 U.S.A.

Integrity Music Limited, a Division of David C Cook
Brighton, East Sussex BN1 2RE, England

The graphic circle C logo is a registered trademark of David C Cook.

Library of Congress Control Number 2012951904
ISBN 978-0-8307-8191-1
eISBN 978-0-8307-8192-8

© 2013, 2021 Gary Thomas
Published in association with Yates & Yates, www.yates2.com.
First edition published in 2013 © Gary Thomas, ISBN 978-1-4347-0489-4

The Team: Michael Covington, Stephanie Bennett, Judy
Gillispie, James Hershberger, Susan Murdock
Cover Design: James Hershberger

Printed in the United States of America
Second Edition 2021

1 2 3 4 5 6 7 8 9 10

011421

*This book is dedicated in celebration of my son
Graham's marriage to Molly on July 12, 2014.*

*May you both grow in grace and love for each
other as you enjoy the blessing of a lifelong love.*

Contents

Acknowledgments

I'd like to thank those who read previous versions of this book and offered many helpful comments: Lisa Thomas, Steve and Rebecca Wilke, Mary Kay Smith, John Card, Steve and Candice Watters, Lindsey Thomas, and Jay Fields. A special thanks is also due to Dr. Ed Young and our home church, Second Baptist in Houston, Texas, for the support base they provide. I am also very grateful to my agents, Curtis Yates and Mike Salisbury of Yates and Yates, for their friendship and partnership for so many years; and to the David C Cook team: Stephanie Bennett and Michael Covington. It's an honor to be part of your team.

For this second edition, I'm grateful to Andi Perkins and Matt Clark for making further suggestions on the update.

A Tale of Two Tears

I'd like to share two true scenarios with you. Together they reveal how crucial it is to make a wise choice about whom you marry.

The first scenario is that of a man whose face grew taut as he confessed, "Let me be honest with you. My marriage has constituted the biggest cross of my life."

The tears that slipped out of this normally reserved man's eyes and rolled down his cheeks provided a sobering picture of the weight this man carries with him every day of his life. Though God has used him in some amazing ways, he said that his marriage acted more like a weight than an encouragement. He keeps moving forward because he believes it's the right thing to do, but he walks his journey with "a rock in his shoe" that hurts him every step of the way. His marital choice didn't *stop* his journey, but it certainly made it more painful.

The second scenario is of a thirtysomething woman who cried an entirely different sort of tears—happy ones. She spoke of her husband's care for her as she suffered more medical challenges before her thirty-fifth birthday than most people will face in a lifetime. She never expected life to be so difficult. But rather than her spouse being "a rock in [her] shoe," her husband has been a rock to hold on to in the storm, a source of tremendous encouragement. He has made her laugh during her darkest days and genuinely makes her feel beautiful when she feels she looks her worst. "Next to Jesus, my husband has been the greatest joy in my life. I can't even imagine where I'd be without him or how I would have faced all that I have without him by my side."

One person is crying tears of pain, working as hard as he can to keep his marriage together, but he compares his relationship to a cross. It saps his strength, but he perseveres.

The other person is also crying, but not because she is struggling through a difficult relationship. She weeps because she is grateful for a man who loves her so well and so wonderfully that she can't imagine life without him.

Tears of pain and tears of joy.

A marriage compared to bearing the cross.

A union compared to a foretaste of heaven.

Ten years after you're married, what kind of tears will you be crying? Will they be the stinging tears of pain or warm tears generated by joy? The reality is, every marriage has plenty of both kinds of tears, but it's also true that some marriages are marked primarily by pain while others are marked primarily by joy. No marriage is easy, but some marriages build each partner up while others tear each partner down. Every marriage takes time and effort, but some marriages sap the spouses' strength while others generate joy and enthusiasm and intimacy.

I'm writing this book because I want you to cry tears of joy on your tenth anniversary. I want you to be able to say, with all sincerity, "Next to becoming a Christian, marrying _____ is the best decision I've ever made."

I am not a psychologist, but I have spent the bulk of my adult life writing and teaching about marriage from a Christian perspective. I have studied the Scriptures and the best books I could find, have talked to hundreds of thousands of couples all over the world via conferences, have pastorally counseled numerous couples, and have done premarital counseling and officiated at the weddings of many. I've given my life to helping people make marriage "work," and here's one thing I've discovered that might surprise you: it's just as important to ask yourself *why* you want to get married as it is to ask *whom* you should marry. It's not that the "who" doesn't matter (in fact, it matters very much); it's just that asking and settling the "why" question *first* will set you up to make a wise choice about the "who." Why do you want to get married? That's what you need to ask before you decide *whom* to marry.

It's a particularly important question because if you make one bad financial investment, you can always start over, but biblical marriage is a one-shot deal. Many Christians believe there are a couple of biblically "accepted" causes for divorce, but these are limited and severe. In most cases, should you become disappointed in your choice, your obligation as a believer will be to work it out instead of walking out and starting over. This fact alone makes it doubly worth the time, effort, and even the heartache of a breakup for believers to make sure they're making a wise decision before they enter into marriage. Once you get married, every evening, every weekend, every holiday, every morning will be marked, for good or for ill, by that relationship.

The person you marry is the last person you'll see every night before you go to sleep. Her face is the first one you will see when you wake up in the morning. His words will encourage or discourage you; her humor will make you laugh in amusement or cry in shame. His body will pleasure you or threaten you; her hands will hold you or hurt you. His presence will be a healing balm or a reminder of all that could have been.

A Better Way

Let's briefly introduce the why of marriage to set you up to make a wise choice about the who.

The three things that lead most people to get married (which will be discussed later in more detail) are romantic attraction, sexual chemistry, and relational compatibility. Why don't these, or even all three of them together, predict future marital happiness and fulfillment?

- **Romantic attraction** can't be sustained, neuro-chemically, over the long haul.
- **Sexual chemistry**, like infatuation, doesn't last. Long-term sexual satisfaction in marriage has far more to do with character, spiritual maturity, and relational health than initial sexual attraction.
- **Relational compatibility** while dating tells you how well you'll get along *when you're on vacation.* It doesn't predict how well you'll handle managing a house, balancing careers, raising kids, or the day-to-day tasks and responsibilities that make up most of married life.

Even though these three realities are poor predictors of marital success, most people, even most Christians, when they experience all three (become infatuated, experience sexual chemistry, and have such a good time while dating), think, *I've found the one! This is it!*

Unfortunately, many find out much later that someone who was a tremendous dating partner turned out to be a disaster (or at least a huge disappointment) as a spouse. Dating and marriage are worlds apart.

Jesus' words in Matthew 6:33—"Seek first the kingdom of God and His righteousness, and all these things shall be added to you" (NKJV)—provide the two most important things to make a marriage work: purpose and character growth. We'll talk about what both elements of this promise mean and how to discern whether they're present. Just know that they constitute *Jesus'* opinion about what leads to fulfillment in life: serving the kingdom of God (not our own selfish aims) and growing in righteousness.

Notice that while this verse contains a command, it's also an exciting promise of a rich and meaningful life: "and all these things shall be added to you." When husband and wife are committed in Christ as their mission, growing together in the Lord, supporting each other in their spiritual walks, raising children in the fear of the Lord, and loving each other out of reverence for God, joy abounds and even miracles can happen. Selfish people become servants. Strangers become intimate friends. Daily life is filled with the fulfilling drama of kingdom building. There are plenty of mistakes, lots of repenting, times of frustration, sickness, and even doubts. But in the end, God's presence prevails, people are transformed, kingdom work is accomplished, and trials are overcome.

The friendship that results from facing all seasons of life together ... creates a bond that no initial sexual attraction or romantic infatuation could ever hope to match.

On the other hand, I've witnessed how miserable people can make each other when they live for themselves. Though their initial sexual attraction might have been off the charts, it is usually only a matter of months until they are saying and doing awful things to each other. There was a time when they couldn't live without each other. Now they can't bear to live together. When they're in the same room, or in the same car, or on the same phone call, they can't stop fighting.

It's made me realize that the old cliché is all too true: a good marriage is the closest two people will ever come to heaven this side of eternity; a bad marriage is the closest two people will ever come to hell.

Such problems usually erupt from trying to build a life together without purpose, without mission, without something that not only establishes a connection but keeps you caring about each other for the next fifty to sixty years.

Can I be honest with you? There isn't a person alive who can keep you enthralled for the next five or six decades. If that person is really funny, really attractive, and you're really infatuated, you can be enthralled for a few years. But selfish people—even wealthy selfish people or beautiful selfish people or famous selfish people— eventually get bored with each other, and the very relationship that once gave them security and life feels like prison and death.

Instead, I want you to have a spiritually enriching marriage, a marriage that spawns life, vibrancy, intimacy, a lifetime of memories with your best friend, and the overwhelming joy of creating a family together (or enjoying your freedom if you don't have kids or they are grown). Family life is such a good life, and intimate marriage is such an amazing gift. The friendship that results from facing all sea- sons of life together, praying together, raising kids together, serving the Lord together, having fun, having sex, suffering heartaches and heartbreaks, overcoming setbacks and learning to deal with disappointments, and growing together through all of them creates a bond that no initial sexual attraction or romantic infatuation could ever hope to match.

The reward for making a wise marital choice is so tremendous that I don't want you to miss it. The consequences of making a foolish marital choice can be so painful and long-lasting that I don't want you to have to endure them.

I cannot overstate how crucial it is to be cautious and discerning in making such an important decision. This is not a time to fall prey to romanticized foolishness. If you remain rooted in Christ, fully engage your mind, and draw on all your resources—God's guidance, Scripture, your family, your church, your sensible friends—and approach this decision with all intention, purpose, and wisdom, you are far more likely to enter a rich, satisfying, and soul-building marriage.

Ask yourself: "Ten years from now, what kind of tears do I want to be crying? Tears of joy or tears of pain? Do I want to be in a marriage that lifts me up or one that drags me down? A union marked by a shared partnership or one where we're hiding from and hurting each other on a regular basis?"

Stick with me and I'll do everything I can to help you be crying tears of joy a decade from now.

Searching Questions

1. Describe a marriage you respect: What is it about the couple that makes you admire their relationship?

2. Ten years after you're married, how do you hope someone will describe your relationship? Write out the ideal description of the relationship you hope to have.

3. Describe some of the marriages you've seen that you definitely do not want to model. What attributes do you hope to avoid?

4. Why do you want to get married?

5. How do you think getting married with the intention of "seek[ing] first the kingdom of God" will change the way you pursue someone to marry, as well as the type of person you might consider?

The Great Exception

Can you help me out here? There must be a version of the Bible out there I haven't read yet, one that has a mysterious exception clause.

I thought I had the bases covered in my research. I've checked out the King James, the English Standard Version, the New King James, the New International Version (both the 1984 and the 2011 editions), the Message, the New Living Translation, the New American Standard, and many others. None of them—not one—contains the exception clause I'm looking for, so if you find it, will you please email me and let me know which version has it? Because apparently, it's the version many singles read.

The exception clause I'm referring to is supposedly found in Matthew 6:33. Here's how it reads in the New King James Version: "Seek first the kingdom of God and His righteousness, and all these things shall be added to you."

The mysterious version I'm looking for, the one I see so many people following and memorizing, goes something like this: "Seek first the kingdom of God and His righteousness, *except when you're choosing someone to marry. In that case, you should follow your emotions, insisting on a thrilling romantic attraction and overall relational compatibility that makes the relationship fun*, and then all these things will be added unto you."

Let me ask you: Do you trust Jesus? Do you believe He truly has your best interests at heart, that He would never mislead you, that if you follow His advice, you're setting yourself up for the best, most-meaningful, and most-fulfilling life imaginable? Can you count on Him to know what He's talking about? Do you think it's possible that the second most important decision you'll ever make—whom you marry—should be based on Jesus' fundamental agenda for our lives: seeking first God's kingdom and righteousness? Do you believe every significant decision we make should be run through this grid? If our choice of marital partner is an exception, what *wouldn't* qualify as an exception? If Jesus' words aren't relevant for such a crucial decision, why would they have any importance for any lesser decision?

Hear this promise: if you will seek first God's kingdom and His righteousness and refuse to compromise on letting that agenda drive your decision regarding whom you choose to marry, you will set yourself up for a much more fulfilling, spiritually enriching, and overall more satisfying marriage. *The degree to which you compromise on this message is the degree to which you put your future satisfaction in jeopardy by opening wide the door to great frustration and even regret.*

Why We Marry

Every month, millions of older people who own cell phones *still* pay thirty to forty dollars to maintain a home phone line, just because they always have. Even though cell phones have rendered landlines all but antiquated, many older people have yet to update their thinking. Calling the phone company is an unchallenged reflex: move to a new place, get a new landline, and keep paying that bill.

You may laugh at your parents for not getting how the world has moved on, but there are a few unchallenged assumptions younger singles are susceptible to as well. Many, perhaps most, blindly accept the belief that they should seek romantic excitement and sexual chemistry above everything else when it comes to choosing someone to marry.

Our culture is still stuck on viewing marriage through the lens of happiness first and foremost—defining happiness by romantic intensity and sexual chemistry. Since the 1960s, sociologists have found a steady progression of young American men and women who demand more and more of love—yet we're getting less and less out of our marriages. In 1967, a study of college-age women found that 76 percent of women said they would marry someone if the man had every trait they were looking for, even if they didn't feel "romantic love" toward him. In more recent research, 91 percent of women said "absolutely not."[1] That's a huge shift. People have been basing their marital decisions on romantic feelings for several generations now, and I'm asking you to be an astute and honest observer: How's that working out for us?

For starters, how many marriages do you see that are truly happy? I'm not talking about marriages that are less than three years old. Tell me—how many people do you know who have been married ten years or longer whose marriages you admire?

Notice the trend: most people marry on the basis of perceived happiness, but few remain very happy for very long. And yet, every year, hundreds of thousands of couples think *they* can be different, so they base their decision *on the same premise*: we "feel" something special, we seem to be happy together, we're generally compatible, so let's get married.

How many failed marriages will it take for us to see that this approach doesn't work? Are you willing to consider that the Hollywood version of "falling in love" might be leading real people astray? That, as powerful as romantic feelings are, they might not be the best reason to marry someone?

Here's just one quick example of how sexual chemistry, apart from any other consideration, can lead us astray. Psychologically, women are more likely to experience romantic love with dominant men (aggressive, extremely confident, take charge, physically imposing), even though dominant men typically demonstrate *less* ability to express the kind of companionship, relational skills, and emotional attachment that women ultimately desire in a lifelong mate.[2] In other words, women, if you simply follow your feelings, you are more likely to fall in love with a guy who will thrill you for twelve to eighteen months as a boyfriend and then frustrate you for five to six decades as a husband.

Guys, on the other hand, are more inclined to experience romantic love with women they are attracted to physically, yet physical appearance is the thing most likely to change in a person's life. Marriage isn't about being young together; it's about growing old together, and bodies change as we get older.

What draws most of us *into* marriage is rarely the ingredient that serves long-term happiness in marriage. Understanding this alone will help you make a wise choice.

Romantic attraction, as wonderful

and as emotionally intoxicating as

it is, can actually lead you astray

as much as it can help you.

Maybe Being in Love Isn't Enough

I had a sobering conversation with a woman my age. She's been divorced twice. She was getting serious with another guy, but her boyfriend's behavior made her cry a couple times a week. He said mean things, and though he wasn't physically violent, he could scare her. To make matters worse, she wasn't sure she could trust him—in fact, she'd overheard him telling another woman on the phone that he still loved her. These were, interestingly enough, the very same issues that had led to the breakup of her first two marriages, so you might think they'd be red flags for her.

There were, of course, several positive aspects about the relationship. He could be thoughtful, supportive, occasionally even poetic—but why was she still in the relationship?

I asked her, "Why do you still want to be with him, given all that you've told me?"

Her response was immediate: "Because I'm in love with him. I genuinely and deeply love him."

I paused to set my tone on "as gentle as possible." This was a minefield, but I was afraid that if I didn't address the situation, this woman could make yet another serious mistake after already experiencing two blown marriages.

"Were you in love with your first husband?" I asked.

"Definitely. I was devastated when he cheated on me and then left me."

"And what about your second husband?"

"Yes. It was different, I think, because he fed some ego needs, but of course, I was in love with him."

"And yet both marriages failed."

"That's right."

I took a deep breath and said, "Maybe feeling like you're in love with someone isn't enough of a reason for you to get married. Maybe you need to find something more. You've tried it twice and it led to much hurt. Are you sure you want to risk it a third time?"

You won't hear a best friend say this in a romantic comedy. Taylor Swift won't sing this and Nicholas Sparks won't write it, but it's true: *just because you're "in love" with someone doesn't mean you should marry that person.* The next chapter will explain why I believe this is true, but for now I'm just throwing it out there and asking you to at least consider that romantic attraction, as wonderful and as emotionally intoxicating as it is, can actually lead you astray as much as it can help you. I agree that "connecting" with someone on that level is a wonderful feeling. Enjoy it, revel in it, even write a song about it if you want, but *don't bet your life on it.*

I've seen infatuation lead far more people astray than into satisfying marriages. I've seen people fail to pursue a relationship, even though they respected, admired, and loved another person because there didn't seem to be that over-the-top, make-my-knees-weak sexual chemistry. And I've watched people rush into a relationship that any objective observer could see had some serious problems on the horizon but the feelings were *so intense*, it all felt *so right*, that two people were willing to bet their lives and their future kids' happiness on it.

Both Scripture and science testify that making a lifetime decision about who to marry primarily on the basis of romantic attraction is a very foolish thing to do.

Searching Questions

1. If you personally know anyone who has gotten married recently, discuss why you think this person got married. Were his or her decisions based on good reasons? What can you learn from watching others?

2. Do you agree that Matthew 6:33 should drive your pursuit of a marriage partner? Why or why not?

3. What would make you consider someone as a potential marriage partner? What would definitely disqualify a person in your mind?

4. What was your reaction to the statement, "Just because you're 'in love' with someone doesn't mean you should marry that person"?

3

Infatuated with Infatuation

The way God made our brains, infatuation resembles an hourglass. The moment you become smitten by someone—the second you find yourself deeply "in love"—that hourglass gets turned over.

There is enough sand in that hourglass, on average, to last you about twelve to eighteen months. Sexual chemistry and romantic attraction can reappear with various degrees of intensity throughout life, but they cease to be the main glue that holds a relationship together on a day-to-day basis. Feelings become "warm and dependable" more than "hot and excitable." God simply did not design our brains to sustain a lifelong infatuation (for some very good reasons).

How do you know if you're in an infatuation? Here are the neurological markers according to Dr. Helen Fisher, a preeminent biological anthropologist who has written on the topic:

- The lover focuses on the beloved's better traits and overlooks or minimizes flaws.
- Infatuated people exhibit extreme energy, hyper-activity, sleeplessness, impulsivity, euphoria, and mood swings.
- One or both partners develops a goal-oriented fixation on winning the beloved.

- Relational passion is heightened, not weakened, by adversity; the more the relationship is attacked, the more the passion grows.
- The lovers become emotionally dependent on the relationship.
- Partners reorder their daily priorities to remain in contact as much as humanly possible, and they even experience separation anxiety when apart.
- Empathy is so powerful that many report they would "die for their beloved."
- Infatuated people think about their lover to an obsessive degree.
- Sexual desire is intense, and the relationship becomes marked by extreme possessiveness.[1]

The way many researchers describe this brain state overall is an "idealization" of the one you love. You focus on strengths (many of which might be imaginary) and are blind to weaknesses (many of which are readily apparent to outside observers). You "idealize" this person to make your beloved the kind of person you *want* him or her to be. It should be clear that in this state you're in no position to make an objective choice if you rely only on your feelings.

Here's what you're dealing with: "Romantic love is involuntary, difficult to control, and impermanent."[2] That's the *psychological* view, but let me say that as Christians—though the initial onslaught of feelings is involuntary—what we do with those feelings, how we control our thoughts, and the level of our obsessiveness is our responsibility. We may not be able to choose the initial onslaught, but we *can* choose how we manage it. We can feed it, starve it, indulge it, or test it.

We are not "evolved mammals" who must play out our biological destiny. We are image bearers of the Creator God, who has redeemed us and given us His Holy Spirit to empower us, correct us, and guide us.

We need to be wise about our human condition but place our hope in our spiritual redemption. It helps Christians to know that romantic love can spring on us unintended and that there is no age limit. You might be single in your twenties or married in your fifties; infatuation will take you through roughly the same emotions and process. Recognizing this, as well as infatuation's impermanence, helps us to be forewarned so that when it happens, we're not caught unprepared. It's a fact of life, but it's going to pass. We all must learn to deal with it and become good stewards of our emotional and relational health.

Infatuated with Infatuation

We live in a culture that is infatuated with infatuation. Psychologists (such as Dr. Helen Fisher and Dr. David R. Hawkins) liken infatuation to an addiction; indeed, it affects the same regions of our brains as cocaine or gambling. Just as some people are more prone to alcoholism than others, some people are more genetically predisposed to "fall in love" more often and more intensely. Infatuation doesn't affect everyone in the same way.

Neurologically, a person's sense of security, self-esteem, spiritual maturity, and personality all affect *how* they fall in love, *what* that experience feels like, and the *intensity* with which they feel those emotions. For example, an insecure person with low self-esteem is likely to be clingy and more obsessive about the relationship than someone who is relatively secure with high self-esteem. A woman from a broken home who has a high fear of abandonment often wants to rush things to "lock in" the relationship, pushing for an early engagement. She's more concerned about avoiding another relational loss than she is about finding the best possible match. Two relatively secure individuals can respect and love each other without experiencing obsessive thinking, euphoric mood swings, or desperate clinginess. The absence of these markers doesn't mean they are less in love than other couples; it might just mean they are more grounded as individuals.

While the experience of infatuation is not the same for any two individuals, when it comes, it is thrilling, powerful, promising, and even transcendent. I don't want to diminish the mystery and poetry of a truly delicious romantic attachment, but in reality you're living through a fairly predictable and observable neurochemical reaction that actually impedes your ability to objectively discern your partner's faults and weaknesses. Dr. Thomas Lewis puts it this way: "Love may not be literally blind, but it does seem to be literally incapable of reason and the levels of appropriate negativity necessary for realism."[3]

Wisdom says we should try to make a relationship work not because we have strong feelings *but because it's a good match.*

A young woman told me that she and her boyfriend were talking about marriage. She asked my advice, and we discussed her boyfriend's strengths. I then asked her about his weaknesses. She blushed a bit and answered, "You know, that's what's so amazing. I don't think he has any."

"Really?"

"I know. I can't believe it either. I guess I just got lucky."

I reminded her of James 3:2, "We *all* stumble in many ways," and said to her, "I'm going to trust the truth of Scripture—that we *all* stumble, including your boyfriend—more than I'll trust your perception. Since you asked for it, my advice is this: don't marry this guy until you can tell me how he stumbles, because I guarantee you—even more than that, *God's Word* guarantees you—that he does stumble, and you might as well know what you're signing up for before you marry him."

Here's the danger of letting these powerful feelings dictate whether you begin, stay in, or end a relationship: when the relationship hits a rough spot (as it inevitably will), most people who have overwhelming feelings will ignore the issues raised by the conflict and try to make the relationship work *because* they have strong feelings. Wisdom says we should try to make a relationship work not because we have strong feelings *but because it's a good match*. Far too often we are more motivated to preserve the relationship if the feelings are there than if the match makes sense. In other words, most of us are motivated more by feelings than by wisdom.

A Predictable Pattern

It's amazing to me how virtually every other tie in life is valued below a new infatuation. A woman asked me to pray for her because she felt like she might "have" to leave the hometown she had lived in for more than twenty-five years—a town where she was gainfully employed, where she had been a church member her entire life, where all her friends and family were.

"Why would you want to leave all this?" I asked.

"I think God may be leading me to," she replied.

It turned out that the motivation was actually a guy, not a God, and one who lived fifteen hundred miles away.

"He must be some guy," I said, "if you're willing to give up everything to follow him. Where did you meet him, if he lives so far away?"

There was a slight pause. "Well …"

"Online?" I suggested.

"Yes."

"So you haven't actually met him in person."

"No. But we've talked on the phone almost every day for weeks."

Let me state up front that I'm not a critic of online dating. Marriage is a good thing, and being intentional about your pursuit of it is commendable, not shameful. Using modern technology to help you is something the church should applaud. But to talk about leaving your entire life behind for someone you've never even met face to face boggles my mind—yet that's how powerful infatuation can be. It can lead us to talk crazy and, even worse, act crazy.

Dr. Helen Fisher believes that romantic attachment is "more powerful than the sex drive."[4] Neurologically speaking, *it's easier to say no to physical sexual passion than it is to regulate the rush of emotional infatuation.* And men, don't think it's only women who read romance novels who are susceptible to this. Because men are attracted to physical appearance more than women are, more men than women experience "love at first sight."

If you've found yourself in the throes of an infatuation and acted foolishly, welcome to the club. A young man I grew up with virtually emptied his bank account trying to buy a woman's affections with expensive dates and elaborate gifts. This normally fiscally minded guy kept believing one more expensive gift, one more costly date, and finally she'd see what an attractive romantic partner he would be. When he ran out of money, she ran out of interest.

Since, according to Dr. Helen Fisher, "romantic love is tenacious and … difficult to control,"[5] once you fall in love, it's hard to fall out of love until the neurochemical reaction fades. Your brain is focused on two tasks during infatuation: *getting* that person and *keeping* him or her. Your brain doesn't have anything left over to evaluate whether someone is *worth* getting or *worth* keeping. The person you're obsessed with can do some awful things, but infatuation is not easily discarded. It'll hang in there and won't let go, despite all evidence that this isn't a person you should be with.

As soon as you become infatuated, you are vulnerable and likely irrational. I say this with all compassion: Don't trust yourself. Recognize what's going on, and set some safeguards (we'll talk about these later). You *can't* be fully objective when infatuation takes root, so don't enter this battle without the guidance of friends, family members, and maybe even pastoral support. You're likely to ignore obvious cues and even defend indefensible behavior.

A quick word to the older readers here. Too many middle-aged people say, "I'm older, I've been married, and I know what I want, so it's okay to cut corners here. We don't need to take the time to get to know each other." That's a dangerous mind-set. No matter how old you are, when infatuation gets hold of your brain, you're just as blind as an eighteen-year-old experiencing his or her first crush.

My wife and I will never forget the regret of a mutual acquaintance who had enjoyed a wonderful marriage for twenty-five years until his wife died. He so missed being married that he started another relationship and was remarried just months after his first wife's funeral—only to realize, not too long later, how different marriage was to a woman of much less character. Never compromise on *whom* you marry just because you want to *be* married.

Vulnerable

Not only are you likely to be somewhat irrational when you're infatuated, but you also become extremely vulnerable. Psychologically, "hearts broken from love lost rate among the most stressful life events a person can experience, exceeded in psychological pain only by horrific events such as a child dying."[6] If you dive in emotionally without knowing whether the person you are falling for is worthy of your trust and that person then cheats on you or rejects you, the fact that he or she is of low character won't remove your pain. You'll still feel tremendous loss.

It's not the same for everyone, of course, but some people have been known to die from a heart attack or stroke following depression caused by a romantic breakup. Neurologically, the pain of social rejection triggers some of the same systems that physical pain does in the brain. Your hurt is real, even though it's emotional.

It is equally dangerous to play with someone else's emotions. One psychologist talked about the horrific price some women pay when they emotionally entangle themselves with a man who doesn't handle a breakup well. Some men react with rage (which is why you don't want to commit to a man until you know him well enough to know he can handle anger without losing his temper): "In our recent studies, we found that an alarming number of men who are unceremoniously dumped begin to have homicidal fantasies.... The loss of love is enough to make a man homicidal."[7]

Take note: "Roughly half of the women who are murdered in America every year are killed by the ones who presumably love them—their husbands, boyfriends, ex-husbands, or ex-boyfriends—in circumstances that are remarkably similar."[8]

Falling in love can be a very dangerous game. Be careful whom you play it with.

And, men, it's just as dangerous to spurn a woman. Some years ago, a Houston woman became so angry when she found her husband with his mistress at a hotel that she ran over him with her car. Still not satisfied, she circled the parking lot and ran over him *again*, pinning him under the car.

Particularly heart-wrenching is that, with the car's tire on top of her husband's body, the woman got out and apologized to him, telling him that she still loved him.[9]

Emotions are powerful things; don't play around with them, and make sure you are with someone who has control over his or her emotions. If I'm going to make myself extremely vulnerable with someone, I want that person to be ruled by the Holy Spirit and able to check those negative thoughts and actions rather than, in biblical language, someone who is ruled by "the flesh."

Wisdom Waits

All of this, I hope, is an argument for not getting married too hastily. Wisdom is patient. Blurting out or acting on your feelings in the bloom of infatuation is a tempting but foolish thing to do: "Do you see a man who is hasty in his words? There is more hope for a fool than for him" (Prov. 29:20 ESV).

One young woman told my friend Virginia Friesen how she had found "the man of her dreams." She and her boyfriend of just three months were already talking about marriage and even discussing a wedding date that would allow just enough time to plan the ceremony. Her boyfriend was "everything she had ever hoped for, and so much different from the last man she dated." Virginia's response was classic and wise, and one I hope you'll consider: "At the three-month mark, my former boyfriend was also everything I had ever wanted. But by month six, the relationship fell apart."[10]

How many of your friends have told you, after being let down by someone they truly loved, "He's not the person I thought he was"? That's a true observation! He *wasn't*. They were relating to an idealized (fictional) version of a man—or woman—not that person's authentic self.

Dr. Fisher has found huge discrepancies between the brain scans of couples who had been in love just about eight months and the scans of those who had been in love about twenty-eight months. Those together just over two years had a far more realistic view of their partner and their relationship than those who were still in the rush of infatuation.[11] But many couples won't wait two years to get married.

The Bible doesn't suggest a time line, and I don't want to create legalistic human rules. I'm more concerned that you progress to the point where you have a reasonably accurate view of someone than that you make it to a certain point on the calendar. Given all that we've looked at, however, I think wisdom says you're being a bit foolish if you get engaged in less than a year. If you get married sooner than that, at the very least you should do so with the blessing of objective and wise friends. On your own, you're making a bet, with lifelong consequences, while in a mind-set that has been proven to be at least somewhat delusional.

Wouldn't you rather be well and happily married for forty-five years than be in a frustrating or loveless marriage for fifty years? I realize five years can sound like a *long time* when you're young and single or brokenhearted and widowed, but breaking up a bad relationship to search for and find a better one will feel like a much better choice in the long run.

Just as it's foolish to let a neurochemical reaction guaranteed to fade in a matter of months lead you to *make* a lifelong decision, it's equally foolish to *reject* marrying someone because you don't feel that short-term infatuation in this relationship. I've heard some say that marrying someone you're not infatuated with is "selling out," but I've also had several readers write to thank me because after reading this book they married someone based on character and mission—without feeling an initial spark—and in hindsight arc very glad they did. Refusing to consider some fine marriage partners simply because the *initial* romantic attachment isn't intense enough is the flip side of *staying* with someone who isn't good for you, simply because the romantic thrill makes it so hard to leave.

Let me put this in another context. Let's say that I, as a man married thirty-six years, "fall in love" with someone other than my wife. Would you say that's reason enough for me to divorce my wife and pursue a romantic relationship with another woman?

I hope not.

But if "falling in love" shouldn't direct my actions as a married man, why should it direct your actions as a single? Marriage doesn't "inoculate" you against future infatuations, by the way. My wife and I read a study that suggests people who stay married for life will become infatuated with six or seven other people during the course of their relationship. That seems like a lot to me. After thirty-six years of marriage, I've been infatuated with others twice; my wife, once. The first time I became infatuated was nearly disastrous because it was unexpected, and I didn't know how to handle it. The second time was easily sidestepped as I realized what was going on and had learned how to respond appropriately.

I'm trying to illustrate that "falling in love" is something to evaluate, not something you should slavishly give yourself over to. Infatuation is a very pleasant, very real brain obsession, but it's a dangerous and false god.

To wrap this up, let me add what we'll discuss in a future chapter: God gives us much freedom in whom we decide to marry. Holding out for that infatuated feeling can be a matter of preference. I have strong opinions on this, but I won't have to live with the person you choose to marry. If you want to hold out for a good match who *also* makes you feel over-the-top infatuated, that's your call. Infatuation or the absence of it isn't what concerns me; the health of the relationship and the wisdom of the match *outside* of the infatuation is.

Searching Questions

1. Describe your first infatuation (if you've had one). Was there a second or third infatuation? In hindsight, do you think the person(s) you became infatuated with was worthy of your romantic attention?

2. Can you relate to what researchers call the "idealization" of someone—giving that person qualities he or she doesn't really have and being blinded to weaknesses? What can people do to protect themselves against this?

3. Have feelings ever led you into a relationship you never should have started? Have the lack of feelings ever led you to end a relationship that should have been given more time? What role do you want romantic feelings to play in future relationships?

4. Have you ever known someone (perhaps yourself) who got into a romantic relationship with a psychologically unhealthy person? How did it end (or how are you still dealing with it now)? What can this teach you about entering into future relationships?

5. What do you believe is a reasonable time frame for two people to progress from meeting each other to becoming engaged? What do you base this on?

4

You May Not Want What You Think You Want

Part of finding the right person to marry is *becoming* the right person, so you might find a bit of inspiration in carefully considering what I'm telling each gender in this chapter. Let me talk to the women first, and then the guys. However, I'd suggest that you read both sections so you can consider the weight of all that I'm suggesting here. And with such a provocative chapter title, let me admit that of *course* I don't know what every man and every woman wants; I'm dealing in popular generalities here to stimulate your thinking and help you critically evaluate what you *should* want.

An Exciting Mistake

Women, my goal is to get you to care about your boyfriend's godliness as much as a wife cares about her husband's godliness. It's his character that will help keep your life mission alive as feelings begin to fade. I've rarely had a wife complain to me about her husband's looks. When wives send me emails, it's *almost always* about character issues.

Yet most women are not seeking men of character first. They are seeking men with whom they feel "in love." If they do feel in love, they will excuse every character fault they see in their man, trying to make the relationship work. If they do not feel in love, they will not seriously consider the man as a potential mate even if he has high character.

Ironically, girlfriends are quick to justify seemingly bad behavior in their boyfriends and try to explain it away, while many wives are eager for everyone around them to know how awful their husbands can be and how everyone should feel sorry for them for having to live with such a wreck of a human being. In fact, not long after they become wives, women will fault men for the very things they overlooked and defended as girlfriends. One woman told counselor Winston Smith, "You don't understand how sick he is! Did I tell you what he did once in college?" Why didn't this episode bother her *before* she got married? Having known this and accepted it, why bring it up now as a wife?

Would that it were the reverse, with girlfriends seriously discussing with their friends their boyfriends' weaknesses so that they could make wise decisions, and wives seriously defending their husbands' honor so that they could cultivate and maintain an intimate marriage. Unfortunately, ignoring your boyfriend's weaknesses and gossiping about your husband's failures are two sure paths to divorce.

In front of a large group, I asked all the married women to stand up. Then I said, "I want you to sit down if you disagree with me that a man's godliness should be one of the top two things a single woman should consider when choosing a mate."

Not one wife—*not one*—sat down. Every married woman was telling every single woman: find a man with solid character who is growing in the Lord and pursuing godliness. That's what those women value most as wives. Yet many single women merely pay lip service to character: "Well, yeah, character and godliness are important, but I think my boyfriend loves God ... in his own way."

Women, ask yourself, What will you most desire in your man ten years from now, when you have kids and a house and are sharing a life together and the infatuation has faded? Find *that*. Look for *that*.

Most married women desire their men to be godly, to have a good sense of humor (life is tough—laughing helps), to be an involved dad, to have a strong work ethic. And yet those four qualities sometimes take a backseat with single women. Some are more attracted to the dreamer who has lots of plans than they are to the workhorse who puts in lots of effort. They value immediate sexual chemistry over a man who keeps his word and lives a respectable life. What so many single women want is a guy who makes their hearts race, their palms sweat, and their sexual chemistry boil, while so many wives want a man they can count on, who will be there for them and their kids every day, and who will faithfully deposit a check in the bank at least once a month.

If you don't deal honestly with this discrepancy—what you value now versus what you'll value ten years from now—you're setting yourself up to live with many regrets. Making a wise marital choice begins with giving proper weight to more significant issues— a shared mission and character traits that will bless you or plague you for the next five or six decades—rather than sexual chemistry or romantic intensity that will fade within months.

It is also easy for women to be carried away by a man's position. Maybe he's wealthy and has an impressive job. Maybe he's a leader in the church. So you make assumptions that because he's this or that, everything else must be okay. Here's the thing: you don't marry a *position*; you marry a *person*. Some wealthy guys are stingy and become unemployed. Some ministry guys are jerks. Don't let a guy's position distract you from his person. You're looking for character, not status; you want to find a man who is solid in his core, not just someone who has an impressive title.

If you're an earnest believer who wants to "seek first the kingdom of God and His righteousness" (NKJV), Acts 6:3 sums up the kind of guy you should look for: "Choose … men … who are known to be full of the Spirit and wisdom." This is what the early church looked for in leaders of their congregations, and it's what you should look for to bring home: men who are filled with the Spirit—they are alive to God, and God is active in them—and men who are full of wisdom. You won't regret making a choice founded on that basis. Can this honestly be said about your boyfriend: "He's a man full of the Spirit and wisdom"?

> If you don't deal honestly with this discrepancy—what you value now versus what you'll value ten years from now—you're setting yourself up to live with many regrets.

A Gorgeous Mistake

And for you guys—since I'm one of you, I know what you're looking for. We like to look, particularly at gorgeous women. Science has established this. A Dutch study demonstrated that attractive women can literally derail a man's cognitive functioning,[1] something the Bible actually concedes, telling young men in Proverbs 31 not to be led astray by a woman's beauty or charm because both of these fade

(v. 30). God knows that we are enthralled with physical beauty. One of those Dutch researchers of the study I just referred to—a published, high-degreed professor—met a stunningly beautiful woman at an academic conference. As they talked, he was eager to make a good impression, but when she asked him where he lived, *he literally could not remember his street address.*[2]

Within marriage, this captivation can be a wondrous thing. It's actually a blessing to be enthralled by your wife's body (Prov. 5:18–19), but when choosing a wife, we also have to be careful about putting more weight on things that last. In case you've never thought about it, a woman's body changes much more rapidly than her character does.

The same is true of sexual chemistry—what launches sexual chemistry won't sustain sexual chemistry. Your girlfriend might very well be all over you (physically) now, but if you're not married, that in itself is a sign of selfishness: when she wants you, when her libido is high, she's enthusiastic and initiating. But if she loved you, if she genuinely cared for you, she would want what's best for you *in Christ.* She would hold back from inappropriate physical intimacy, as she wouldn't want to taunt you or tempt you or pull you away from God.

I can't tell you how many times I've seen this. It's so sad to speak with guys who think their sexually active girlfriends will be sexually active wives just because in the early days of the relationship, when the sexual chemistry was so high, the only problem was reining in the affection, not expressing it. In fact, however, it's often the reverse. If your dating relationship is sustained by sin, what will sustain your marriage? If your girlfriend acts selfishly as a girlfriend, why do you think she won't act selfishly as a wife?

The same sin that moves your girlfriend to get *too* physical before marriage is the sin that will kill or perhaps maim sexual intimacy *after* marriage. Sin, by definition, is overturning God's created order. In God's created order, there should be no sex outside of marriage and lots of fulfilling, generous sex during marriage. Why do you think a person will disobey God in the first instance but obey Him in the second? Doesn't it make sense that if you shut out God to do what you want to do in one season, you'll keep doing it in the next season?

That's why, when choosing a wife, you want to find a woman who is seeking first God's kingdom *now*. You want to find a woman who is seeking righteousness *now*. If she isn't a mission-based woman while you date, what will make her a mission-based woman after the wedding?

Your best chance at sexual satisfaction in marriage is not to focus on appearance alone but rather to find a woman of virtue. Proverbs 31 describes her as a woman who "fears the LORD" (v. 30). When a woman is motivated by kindness, compassion, generosity, and understanding; when she is good at forgiving (because *every* husband needs plenty of forgiveness); when she is desirous to serve as Jesus models service, she's going to be a very satisfying sexual partner and an overall kind wife as well.

In other words, without discounting how intoxicating beauty can be, marry a woman whose character you respect, whose strengths and gifts you admire, and whose spiritual walk in the Lord is something you want to emulate.

Proverbs 12:4 warns young men, "A wife of noble character is her husband's crown, but a disgraceful wife is like decay in his bones." If you've ever seen someone slowly waste away of cancer, that phrase—"a disgraceful wife is like decay in his bones"—should strike fear in your heart. You will be eaten from the inside out when you attach yourself to a foolish woman, however beautiful (or rich or charming) she may be.

I've met men who credit their current walk with God to being married to strong Christian women who inspire them and who wouldn't put up with spiritual apathy or immaturity. These men confess that they shudder when they think of how they might have fallen if not for the spiritual strength, wisdom, and example of their wives.

I love being married to a beautiful woman; it's a blessing I won't even try to deny. But I *treasure*, even more, being married to a godly woman.

Here's the reality: many women are led into marriage primarily by romantic idealism, and many men are swept to the altar by sexual attraction (this is obvious stereotyping and may not be true of you—it can go both ways). To make a wise marital choice, rid yourself of inferior motivations. The wrong *why* will lead you to the wrong *who*.

Fleeting Fun

Let's compare what the world values with what Jesus teaches. The world values a brief, intense, romantic attraction that makes us both vulnerable and irrational and that lasts, on average, about twelve to eighteen months. It evaluates "love" by the intensity of an emotional attachment that science tells us won't last. This is the fleeting love celebrated in most movies, novels, and songs. You've been conditioned to value it above all else and have been told that it's the only "authentic" love.

In *Titanic*, when Rose's new boyfriend, Jack, says running away together doesn't make any sense (especially since they have known each other for less than seventy-two hours), Rose responds, "It doesn't make any sense. That's why I trust it."[3] With just the right music in the background, this might make for a compelling scene, but it almost always creates a grief-ridden life.

In contrast, Jesus taught us to base our decisions on the eternal: seeking God's kingdom and His righteousness. Jesus' words urge us to find someone with whom we can share a mission instead of an emotional infatuation. Instead of telling us to find someone who makes us lose all sense of objectivity, Jesus' teachings direct us to make a decision that will lead to righteousness—to seek someone who will inspire us toward godliness, who will confront us when we go astray, who will forgive us when we mess up, who can encourage us with wisdom when we are uncertain about how to proceed.

If we are spiritually healthy, this is the life we desire. This is the life that leads to a growing joy, not a fading attachment. The crucial "third stage" of relationship—beyond sexual desire and romantic attachment—is long-term affection. This bond is best fostered through friendship and a shared mission. It lasts until death and, unlike romantic infatuation, gets deeper with age. Time serves intentionally cultivated intimate affection, even as it kills infatuation.

Jesus' words—indeed, the whole of Scripture—call God's people to build a spiritual partnership. That's what you should be looking for: Can this person walk with me toward God? It's not selfish to choose wisely in marriage; it's being a good steward of the one life God has given you. If you marry someone with serious mental issues, addictions, or character flaws, it's like entering a marathon with a heavy backpack. Ask yourself, Will the person I'm considering help me run the race God has laid out before me, or will he or she act like an anchor dragging at my feet?

Granted, the marriage choice is different from simply choosing a partner or friend. If there is no sexual attraction, you're going to have a difficult time fulfilling your role as a husband or wife. If the thought of seeing this person naked makes you want to vomit, don't marry him or her. Sex is a significant aspect of marriage, and if you don't think you can enjoy and enthusiastically participate in sexual relations, you shouldn't get married. In the long-term, however, sexual intimacy dies in most marriages due to relational issues more than a lack of physical attraction. Two people who genuinely care for each other, are kind to each other, share a mission together, and want to grow together naturally feel a desire to be sexually intimate.

In other words, there is *more* to think about when choosing a marriage partner than Matthew 6:33 covers, but there should never be *less* than that. If the person you are interested in is not someone with whom you believe you can seek first God's kingdom and pursue a life of righteousness, I think you're settling for second best, at least from the perspective of what Jesus says is most important in life.

Searching Questions

1. What are some character traits that might be fine in a boyfriend or girlfriend but unacceptable in a husband or wife?
2. Is it realistic to ask people to consider a person's character above intense romantic feelings? How does one learn to do this?
3. Women, do you think there are any discrepancies between what you'll desire in a husband and the kind of guy who interests you as a boyfriend? Discuss these.
4. Men, how important do you think it is to base your decision to marry someone on her character over her physical appearance? How do you balance this?
5. List five things the world typically values in romantic relationships, and then contrast them with what the Bible suggests makes up true and lasting love.

5

Soul Mate or Sole Mate?

A young woman admitted that the man she was dating was—for lack of a better word—a jerk. He had cheated on her with her best friend, he had no aspirations, and any objective person could see that the guy she had fallen for was not suitable marriage material. Still, she persisted in her devotion: "I know I can't trust him, I know he doesn't treat me very well, I know he's not going anywhere—but ... but ... I think he may be *the one*."

She recognized marrying him would be a disaster because, frankly, *dating* him had been a disaster. But if you believe there's only one right person for you, and that person just happens to be a selfish loser, what else are you supposed to do?

This notion that there is just one person who can, in the words immortalized in a famous movie scene, "complete us"[1] is a perilous mind-set with which to approach a lifelong marital decision. Yet it seems to be the majority opinion. Studies show that most singles are in a somewhat desperate search for their "soul mate." One Rutgers University study found that 94 percent of single women in their twenties say that the first requirement in a spouse is that he's a soul mate, someone with whom they feel an almost cosmic connection. Just as surprising, 87 percent think they'll actually find that person "when they are ready."[2]

Blame Zeus

The origins of this "soul mate" line of thinking are so bizarre you'll hardly believe it. Over two thousand years ago, the Greek philosopher Plato surmised that there was once a "super race" of androgynous humans that attempted to overthrow the gods. This super race consisted of "round" people, comprising both male and female in one person, and, in that state, they were getting too powerful. So Zeus said, "I shall now cut each of them in two, ... and they will be both weaker and more useful to us through the increase in their numbers."[3]

The forceful cutting in two supposedly left both halves desperate to be reunited. When the two halves did finally find each other, all they could do was cling to each other, which led to their deaths "because they were unwilling to do anything apart from one another."[4] Zeus saved the day—deprived and desperate humans are no longer so powerful and no longer such a threat to the gods.

Notice, however, that in Plato's view, romantic love makes us weaker, whereas in the biblical view, love makes us stronger. What is your love doing to you: Are you stronger because of it, or do you feel more vulnerable, weak, and perhaps even desperate?

Infatuation can lead us down the path of desperation, can't it? You feel so connected to someone that you can't bear to be apart, even for a few hours. You feel vulnerable in a whole new way. Life apart from the relationship feels so unimportant that it virtually stops. Well, Plato figured that's because there was a time when you weren't apart and therefore can't function on your own.

He went on to suggest,

> So it is really from such early times that human
> beings have had, inborn in themselves, Eros for
> one another—Eros, the bringer-together of their

ancient nature [i.e., man and woman as one being], who tries to make one out of two and to heal their human nature. Each of us, then, is a token of a human being, because we are sliced like fillets of sole, two out of one; and so each is always in search of his own token.[5]

True Human Nature

A scriptural view of human nature couldn't be more different. According to the Bible, our problem is not that we've been sliced apart from an ancient human half but that we have been separated from God by our sin and need to be reconciled to God through the work of Jesus Christ on the cross. Once we are reconciled to God, He brings us together as humans. Marriage is a wonderful, even glorious reality, but it is secondary to our spiritual identity as children of God and something that won't even exist in heaven (Matt. 22:30).

Our search for a life mate, then, isn't one of desperation, but rather one of patiently looking for someone with whom we can share God's love and live out God's purpose.

Plato's "soul mate" philosophy circumvents the concept of applying wisdom and replaces it with trying to mystically discern whether you are "meant to be" with someone. For every person who stumbles into a sensible matching with this guidance, there are a dozen who act foolishly and hastily. For starters, how do you know if someone is your destined soul mate? Most typically, people try to discern it through their feelings. They sense a connection unlike anything they've ever known before. But we've already established that infatuation is powerful, all-consuming—*and short-lived*.

Some well-meaning believers might try to say, "I asked God," and while I applaud your pursuit of heavenly guidance, can I at least question your objectivity and ability to discern God's voice when your brain is obsessed with getting and keeping someone with whom you've fallen into a deep infatuation?

Discerning someone's character, values, and suitability for marriage is *hard work*. It takes time, counsel, and a healthy dose of objective self-doubt. Identifying someone as "God's chosen" or Plato's "soul mate" is comparatively easy. You "feel" it in your gut. It *seems* right. You can't imagine anyone else. You must have found *the one*!

Such individuals may marry on an infatuation binge without seriously considering character, compatibility, life goals, family desires, spiritual health, and other important concerns. Then when the infatuation fades and the relationship requires work, one or both partners suddenly discover they were "mistaken." This person must not be their soul mate after all; otherwise, it wouldn't be so much work. Next, they panic. Their soul mate must still be out there! Such people can't get to divorce court fast enough, lest someone steal their "one true soul mate" meant only for them.

The sad reality is that when we get married for trivial reasons, we will seek divorce for trivial reasons. We need something much more lasting on which to base a lifelong commitment—one that even has eternal implications.

Let me ask you a tough question: If someone is willing to marry you without doing the hard work of determining whether you're suitable to be his or her spouse and the parent of your future kids, what makes you think this person will do the hard work of building a satisfying, God-honoring marriage? The *way* someone chooses to get married is a good indicator of the way he or she will stay married after the wedding takes place in order to make the marriage grow.

Are You Trying to Replace God?

Take a deep breath. Your marital choice is crucial, but it will *never* define you. If you are a believer, God—not your marital status or marital happiness or frustration—defines your life. Let the pursuit of marriage be one of joy, one you undertake with your closest eternal companion—God Himself—walking with you.

You're not trying to replace God by finding your perfect match—that's desperation. You are already perfectly loved and looking for someone who can help you grow in and share that love—that's security. Christians should never be defined as *desperate*. We are well loved, well cared for, cherished by the One who knows us best, and secure in His acceptance, love, affirmation, and purpose.

On the other hand, while it can be a tremendous ego boost to have someone seem like he or she is desperate for you, ask yourself if you're willing to play the role of God in that person's life. One young woman once told me (when I was single), "I could never be happy without you." When I talked this over with my campus pastor, he helped me see that this was a red flag. It initially felt nice to be so wanted and needed, but he explained how someone who says this of another human being isn't in a right relationship with God. Did I want to join my future with someone who allowed God to have such a small role in her life that another fallen human would forever determine her happiness?

Before we can go on, you need to wrestle with this question: Do you believe there is only one right person to marry? Perhaps you reject Plato's soul-mate line of thinking but have developed a "Christian alternative," something along the lines of finding the one person whom God created "just for you."

If so, how do you justify that biblically? Let's look at the evidence.

Wisdom over Destiny

The language of the Bible doesn't suggest there is only one right choice for marriage. Rather, all the teaching passages seem to suggest that there are wise and unwise choices. We are encouraged to use wisdom, not destiny, as our guide when choosing a marital partner.

Proverbs takes a supremely pragmatic approach: "A wife of noble character *who can find*?" (31:10). This verse assumes that we are involved in a serious pursuit, actively engaging our minds to make a wise choice. And the top thing a young man should consider is this: "Charm is deceptive, and beauty is fleeting; but a woman who fears the LORD is to be praised" (Prov. 31:30). The Bible tells young men to search for a woman of character; while looks won't last, godly character improves with age. It says absolutely nothing about "feelings" and warns against putting too much emphasis on physical attraction or social grace. Instead, *this verse makes a woman's faith the defining characteristic of her suitability to be an excellent wife.*

I can speak from experience: nothing compares to being married to a godly woman. Kindness, generosity, spiritual companionship— these all grow deeper and truer and more pleasant over time. But I know from counseling far too many troubled marriages that there is also nothing more tedious and exhausting than being married to a stunningly beautiful but narcissistic woman.

You can take this too far; as I already stated, I'm not suggesting you marry someone in whom you have no sexual interest at all. But the first priority, according to Scripture, is to find a spiritually compatible person, and *then*, under *that* umbrella, find a *sexually* compatible person. If you reverse those two categories, you can expect to find short-term satisfaction at the risk of long-term frustration. Let the why of marriage point you to the who, and don't let a suave and handsome who change your reason why.

When we jump forward to the New Testament, there is no hint at all about finding "the one person" that God created "just for you." It's far more a pragmatic choice: Do you think you'll sin sexually if you don't get married (1 Cor. 7:2)? Are you acting improperly toward a woman you could marry (v. 36)? If so, go ahead and get married—it's your choice, and God gives you that freedom. But notice this: the choice is made *on the basis of seeking righteousness*. "Do you think you might keep sinning if you stay single? Then get married."

In helping people wrestle with the decision to marry, the apostle Paul admitted there are benefits to singleness and benefits to being married. If you're unable to handle sexual temptation as a single, Paul said, then by all means get married. This is a clear call to base your marital decision on the desire to live a more righteous life, knowing that without marriage you might fall into unrighteous living.

Of course, Paul isn't talking about *when* to get married or *whom* to marry here. His distinction is a more general one about being married or not being married at all. It would be a serious misreading to suggest that if you wrestle with sexual temptation you should rush forward and marry the first person who is willing to marry you. This is general advice, not specific advice.

Paul also left the decision of *whether* to get married up to us in verses 8–9: "To the unmarried and the widows I say: It is good for them to stay unmarried, as I do. But if they cannot control themselves, they should marry."

Paul was simply modeling the pragmatic approach of Jesus, who spoke matter-of-factly about people who were born eunuchs and others who "choose to live like eunuchs for the sake of the kingdom of heaven" (Matt. 19:12). Did you get that word *choose*? Jesus says it's a *choice*. It is not wrong if you want to get married; it is not wrong to want to stay single. The Bible clearly says we shouldn't feel forced to marry or feel prohibited from marrying; this is one of those life decisions God leaves up to us. But God *does* care about *why* we decide to marry and the kind of person we marry.

The crowning piece of our argument, however, the one the "Christian Platonists" are going to have a difficult time overcoming, is Paul's advice in 1 Corinthians 7:39. Paul clearly left the choice of marriage up to us in the most explicit of terms: "She is free to marry anyone she wishes, but he must belong to the Lord." Did you catch that? *She is free to marry anyone she wishes* as long as the man she "wishes" belongs to the Lord. Could Scripture be any plainer?

It is our choice *whether* we want to get married and *whom* we want to marry. In other words, *you get to choose*. This isn't a denial of God's providence, nor does it preclude God leading two people together in certain cases. Rather, it's the Bible's way of saying that while marriage is important, God has given you an awesome responsibility, so choose wisely.

The reason it is so crucial to adopt
the Bible's view of a wise choice over
"finding the one" is that the Bible's
approach encourages you to objectively
consider the person you plan to marry.

The lazy and overly mystical might resent this teaching. They might say, "That's not fair, God—just tell me who to marry, and I'll get married." That's an immature attitude. God created both men and women to be ruling agents (Gen. 1:28), and as redeemed Christians, we will rule again in eternity (1 Cor. 6:2–3). The ability to rule is something we grow into, and marriage is a golden opportunity to develop the discernment and discretion we need to become fully functioning regents in God's kingdom work.

The need to find "the one" is based in desperation—as if, apart from that "one," we lack something. The Bible views us as recipients of God's perfect love, already charged with an important life mission (seeking first the kingdom of God), and thus the decision to marry, though crucial, won't define us. Nor will *whom* we marry define us. It's sort of like this: medical wisdom says you need to exercise and eat right to be at your best. How you exercise—whether you ride a bike, swim, or jog—is up to you. Just exercise. The Bible says we need to live a righteous life, including how we handle our sexual and emotional desires, seeking first the kingdom of God above all else. How we do that—whether as singles or marrieds, whether pursuing an introverted bookworm or an extroverted athlete to be a life partner—is up to us.

In all honesty, this is a check on those who make too much of marriage. Making too much of marriage is to make too little of our relationship with God. And when we make too little of our relationship with God, we undercut our source of love, which makes success in marriage less likely. Focusing on marriage too much is, ironically enough, the best way to kill it.

Find a partner with whom you can seek first the kingdom of God, someone who inspires you toward righteousness, and when you do, "all these things will be added to you."

Making the Choice

The reason it is so crucial to adopt the Bible's view of a wise choice over "finding the one" is that the Bible's approach encourages you to objectively consider the person you plan to marry. There is no objective measurement of "destiny." How, indeed, can you possibly know if someone is your soul mate? When we adopt the biblical attitude of making a wise choice, we can use all God has given us to arrive at a solid decision that should be based on a number of questions:

> • *Scriptural Mandates*
> Is the person a believer who fears God? (Prov. 31:30)
> Is he or she biblically eligible for marriage?
>   (Mark 10:11–12)
>
> • *Wisdom*
> How does this person handle money?
>   (Prov. 31:16, 18)
> Is this person a hard worker? (Prov. 13:4; 26:13–15)
> Does he or she live an upright life?
>   (Prov. 13:6, 20; 25:28)
> Does this person wound people with words, or is this
> an encourager? (Prov. 12:18; 18:21)
> Is this person peaceful or quarrelsome?
>   (Prov. 17:19; 29:8)
>
> • *Parental and Pastoral Advice*
> Proverbs 15:22 tells us, "Plans fail for lack of counsel, but with many advisers they succeed."
> Do the people you most respect have serious reservations about the relationship?

- *Prayer*

    Accepting the fact that God leaves the choice up to us (1 Cor. 7:39) shouldn't prevent us from seeking His wisdom in prayer. List biblical priorities for a solid marriage partner, and put each one before God. *Wait* and *listen* to see if God brings anecdotes and examples to your mind that either confirm or challenge your decision to get married.

Grappling with all of the above may not sound romantic, but it is not antiromance. It's entirely possible to become infatuated with someone you would be very wise to marry. The difference is, you're not marrying this person *because* you're infatuated. And hopefully, you're not completely discounting other possibilities simply because you're *not* feeling infatuation.

Instead of a "soul mate," I'd like to suggest a more biblical pursuit; you need to look for a "sole mate." It sounds exactly the same, but the meaning is radically different.

What Is a Sole Mate?

A sole mate is someone who *walks* out with us (the "sole" of a shoe) the biblical command to seek first the kingdom of God. The most accurate definition of true love is found in John 15:13: "Greater love has no one than this: to lay down one's life for one's friends."

Rather than based on feelings, this love is based on sacrifice. The Bible calls men to act like martyrs toward their wives, laying down their own lives on their wives' behalf (Eph. 5:25). Titus says older women need to train younger women how to love their husbands (Titus 2:3–4). Need I point out, men and women, that these are *severe* verses? Martyrdom on behalf of your wife? Being "trained"—actively studying and learning—how to love your husband? This is heavy stuff.

Guys, you may feel infatuated now, but in agreeing to become a husband of one wife, you are agreeing to put her needs above your own for the rest of your life regardless of what happens. Are you ready for that? And women, as soon as you say "I do," you are committing before God and the community of faith to expend your best efforts helping, loving, and supporting this man. Infatuation fills your eyes with what you're *getting*, but let the Bible fill your mind with what you're committing to *give*.

These passages don't deny the joy of romance in a healthy marriage (as we'll discuss later), but they do make clear that love in marriage, as God defines it, is not merely an emotion; it's a policy and a commitment that we choose to keep in the harshest of circumstances.

Christian life is a journey toward love, growing in love, expanding in our ability to love, surrendering our hearts to love, and increasingly becoming a person who is motivated by love. A "sole mate" appreciates that marriage is a partnership committed to the task of walking out the biblical mandate to always put love first. It's not marked by the couple who displays the most emotion, with the biggest smiles on their faces, who can't keep their hands off each other, but rather, the women or men who, through the duties and sacrifice of marriage, have trained themselves to love with God's love. They walk out the gospel on a daily basis, forgiving, serving, and putting others first in the most ordinary issues of life in such a way that they see themselves in training for godliness. Such a couple will grow together, as surely as merely sentimental couples will grow apart.

I knew Lisa could be a sole mate for me before we got married because she was eager to memorize entire books of the Bible with me. We went to the same Christian concerts but often didn't sit together because we were each bringing nonbelieving friends. Lisa was as committed to walking in obedience as I was when it came to physical affection. She believed in discipling others (actively leading a small group), so I knew she'd have the same focus as a mom. She went on a summer mission trip that I didn't go on (I had to work for the money to get through college). That told me she was sold out to serving Jesus whether or not I was with her. In fact, it told me that she was willing to sacrifice a summer of dating for a summer of service. That made her more attractive to me, not less.

I was very attracted to Lisa physically, but frankly, I could probably have been physically attracted to dozens of women on our college campus. The difference was that Lisa was proving herself to be a sole mate like few others, and I was overjoyed when she agreed to become my wife.

I didn't fully realize back then how important all this was. While I am still very attracted to Lisa, the backbone of our relationship is a joint pursuit of God's truth, a commitment to travel God's journey of sacrificial love, and a commitment to grow in godliness. Laughing now, Lisa said when she married me she thought I "could do no wrong." After we got married, she found out otherwise—and was relieved that I was as motivated to *keep* growing spiritually as she was.

Seeking first God's kingdom and righteousness together may not sound like the most *exciting* or *emotional* love, but it is certainly the *truest* love. And it is the only kind of love that lasts.

Searching Questions

1. Do you believe there is just one person you're "supposed" to marry? What do you base this belief on? How will this affect the way you approach finding a marriage partner?

2. Discuss this statement: "Notice, however, that in Plato's view, romantic love makes us weaker, whereas in the biblical view, love makes us stronger." Compare the two views on love.

3. In what ways do you think the process someone uses to get married (rushed or deliberate) reflects whether he or she will put in the relational work necessary to make a marriage succeed and continue to grow ever more intimate throughout the years?

4. Why is it dangerous to date when you feel desperate? How can someone deal with such desperation responsibly so that it doesn't affect the choice of marriage partner?

5. Do you agree that the mystical approach of asking God to just tell you whom you "should" marry is an immature way to approach getting married? Why or why not?

6. How might the "sole mate" notion of love—marriage being designed not to complete us but to provide us with a life partner with whom we can grow in our ability to love—affect whom you consider marrying?

6

A Match Made in Heaven?

When I tell large groups that we shouldn't assume God has chosen one person just for us, I often hear in response, "What about Isaac and Rebekah?" This is a tremendous love story. What understanding can we can gain from this narrative?

In Genesis 24 we read that Abraham sent his servant to find a suitable wife for his son Isaac. Abraham was getting old and increasingly concerned that his son didn't have a wife and thus no heir. Many important promises hinged on Isaac producing an heir.

Abraham's servant prayed for success: "LORD, God of my master Abraham, please grant me success today, and show kindness to my master Abraham" (Gen. 24:12 NASB).

This is the *first* time in Scripture that we read of someone asking God for specific guidance. From all the rest of Scripture, we naturally assume that part of prayer is seeking guidance, but this is the first recorded instance of prayer being used in that way. And this first recorded instance seeks guidance for making a *wise marital choice*.

From this we can deduce that it is not wise to reduce the marital decision-making process to reason alone. Wise decision-making is to be applauded, but it is entirely appropriate to seek God's discernment, to listen to His voice, to let Him give us some feedback on our inclinations. We may get no confirmation or warning—but it is wise to give God an opportunity to do just that and even to hope and expect that He will guide us and help us in our pursuit.

Kind Women Only Need Apply

Look not only at the fact that Abraham's servant prayed but also at *what* he prayed for:

> Behold, I am standing by the spring, and the daughters of the men of the city are coming out to draw water; now may it be that the young woman to whom I say, "Please let down your jar so that I may drink," and who answers, "Drink, and I will water your camels also"—may she be the one whom You have appointed for Your servant Isaac; and by this I will know that You have shown kindness to my master. (vv. 13–14 NASB)

The "mystical" way to read this is to suggest that the woman's response was neutral except to serve as a sign: she was saying the right words. Another way to understand them is that Abraham's servant asked God to let the woman He had chosen be the kind of woman who was described in this prayer ("may she be the one ..."). Such a woman would have had to be extraordinarily generous and kind. Each camel could drink up to *twenty-five gallons of water*. Asking God to choose a woman who was willing to draw up that much extra water, for *ten* camels, when the water had to be pulled up by bucketloads (there were no faucets on a well), on the heels of a comparatively minor request (one man's thirst), would be abnormally generous, well beyond the bounds of common civility and certainly way beyond any cultural expectations of hospitality.[1]

Abraham's servant wasn't just asking for a sign; he was asking for a woman of character who would be one in a thousand. He clearly wanted his master's son to have a wife who would bless him with hospitality, so he wanted a woman who would go well above a simple request. The Bible praises Rebekah's beauty and purity (v. 16), but the servant was seeking a woman who was uncommonly kind and generous. That's what he wanted for Isaac.

And that's exactly what we've been talking about: find that person whose character shines above all others.

A Chosen Family

When seeking to apply this to your own life, consider the following: God's purpose in establishing a union between Isaac and Rebekah required her to be of a certain nationality. That is no longer the case for us when choosing a spouse (Gal. 3:28). Instead, the Bible instructs us to find a person of a common *faith*, not common ancestry. Furthermore, God had specially chosen Abraham's family to bless the entire earth; while God has also chosen us to build His kingdom, Isaac's place in history was a special calling, unique to his pure bloodline, particularly as it related to producing certain heirs that would result in the birth of the Messiah. New Testament reproduction isn't about blood*lines* but rather blood *application* (the cross of Christ).

Also keep in mind that Old Testament narratives aren't always normative. The Old Testament describes what happened, but that doesn't mean we should copy what happened, especially since the Old Testament isn't always explicit about denouncing clearly inappropriate actions. While God clearly blessed the union of David and Bathsheba with the birth of Solomon, it would be a monstrosity of application to suggest that adultery and then a covered-up murder is an acceptable method for meeting and choosing a mate. Likewise, no one would suggest that a widow should search for a man twice her age, work in his field, and uncover the man's feet in the middle of the night to offer marriage, as Ruth did with Boaz. Yet, indisputably, these became significant unions and families in the genealogy leading up to the birth of the Christ.

The story of Isaac and Rebekah is an account of what was but not necessarily of what should be for all God's people. Just because there may have been one ordained wife for Isaac doesn't mean there is one ordained wife for *you*. If you think this passage is normative—that it should direct how you look for a spouse—apply it accurately and fully. Ask your dad to hire someone to go find your future mate and agree to marry that person sight unseen. That would be a true and complete application, and I haven't heard of many who would be willing to do that!

Of course, it's entirely possible that God may have a person He particularly desires you to marry. It is certainly within a reasonable understanding of God's working through history to believe that He can create and call two people together under His providence to accomplish a particular work. But even if that's the case in your life, how can you discern such a calling? I believe the wise response is to apply everything we've been talking about. Since God wants your best, I don't believe He's likely to "match" you with someone who is of low character. Of course, pray that God will help you make a wise decision, and even that He'll bring a suitable partner into your social network (or open your eyes to someone who's already in it). That's living by faith and asking for God's help. But don't try to justify an unwise choice by claiming divine sanction. You risk pitting the wisdom of God against the call of God, and that's a dangerous place from which to make a lifelong decision.

According to the full account of

Scripture, for the vast majority of us,

whether we marry, and whom we marry,

falls under God's permissive will.

Some people seek "God's will" primarily as a shortcut. They don't want to do the hard work of finding and testing out a suitable mate, so they seek a mystical or emotional sign that "this is the one." That's foolish. Mystical leadings and emotional connections are confusing at best and a deplorable foundation on which to base a monumental decision.

This is not to suggest that God doesn't occasionally work "outside the box"—I'm being as balanced as I can be here. For example, it was clearly God's will for Joseph to take Mary as his wife (Matt. 1:20–25). If God appears to you in a dream and says that He is fulfilling prophecies through your future marital union, and you can be sure that it really is God speaking, marry that person! But I doubt that God will give most of us such a certain and extremely specific direction. According to the full account of Scripture, for the vast majority of us, whether we marry, and whom we marry, falls under God's permissive will.

Throughout the remainder of the book we will continue the work of helping to equip you to make a supremely *wise* marital choice.

Searching Questions

1. The start of Isaac and Rebekah's story teaches us to cover the process of choosing a mate with prayer. How big a role has prayer played in your own pursuit?

2. How can the *content* of Abraham's servant's prayer—searching for an extraordinarily kind partner for his master's son—direct our own prayers for a future spouse?

3. If someone truly believes that God is calling him or her to marry a *particular* person, what are some reasonable tests of that calling?

4. How can the story of Isaac and Rebekah direct our own marital pursuit? In what ways is the story *not* relevant for today's believers?

7

Walk toward the Music

"When it comes to choosing a mate, God will bring the right person to me at the right time. I'll just sit back and wait."

That sounds so spiritual, so trusting, so ... holy.

But consider this attitude in virtually any other aspect of life. For instance, how "holy" and wise does this sound: "I don't plan to apply to any colleges. I figure if I'm supposed to go to college, God will make sure the University of Texas sends me a letter, complete with a dorm key. That'll be my sign."

Or this: "Why should I fill out a job application? If God wants me to work at Microsoft, He can have the CEO give me a call."

If someone spoke like that, you'd think that person was a religious fanatic. But we put the language of dating and finding a mate into similar "Christianese" and it sounds so noble: "Don't worry about finding someone to marry. If you just focus on God, He'll bring someone along at exactly the right time." There are some very disappointed people in their thirties and forties who lived by this philosophy and now fight resentment toward God because they still aren't married. After all, wasn't He supposed to bring their future spouses right to their doorsteps?

Just as troublesome, many people show open disdain for anyone who goes to college in part hoping to find someone to marry or who even seems intentional in pursuit of marriage. I'm a firm believer in a good education, but let's be honest: many people will never use the degrees they get from college. That doesn't mean the degrees and experience of learning aren't valuable—they certainly are—but the person you marry will have a far greater impact on your life satisfaction than your major (or lack of one, if you choose not to go to college) ever will. What's so wrong with spending four years trying to find a suitable life mate—perhaps not as the main goal of college but certainly one of the top goals? Or, if you're not a college student, what's wrong with attending a church that offers many opportunities to meet eligible men and women your age?

That's what Austin did! He fell "head over heels" in love with a young woman named Madeline, but it took Madeline some time to warm up to him. To give her more time, Austin started going to her church. That was forty years ago, and they're still married today, a happy union that began with an active and intentional pursuit. If Austin had waited for God to remind Madeline about Austin, both Austin and Madeline admit they never would have gotten together.

Of course, you can take this advice too far. I'm not suggesting that you put your life on hold and give only cursory attention to your studies or job until you find someone to marry. You don't want to shortchange your education or other social opportunities (like making lifelong friends). I'm merely suggesting you keep your eyes open.

Some women are hesitant to be intentional because they want the man to pursue *them*. What I'm suggesting doesn't contradict that; however, are you putting yourself in situations where you can be pursued? Are you in a place where you can be noticed? Can you do anything to put yourself in somebody's awareness?

Walk toward the Music

My wife and I arrived in Baden-Baden, Germany, late on a summer evening. Our hotel sat in the middle of a pedestrian district that, except for a couple restaurants and gelato parlors, shut down by 8:00 p.m. We weren't ready to call it a night and wondered what we should do.

In the distance, I could barely hear the faint sound of some music. "Hey," I suggested, "let's walk toward the music. Something must be going on."

Boy, was there! About a quarter mile away social energy buzzed as an outdoor concert serenaded twelve to fifteen makeshift restaurants just outside Baden-Baden's famous casino. The small festival welcomed all the tourists who were there for the horse races that weekend. Apparently, one of the reasons the pedestrian area was drained of all activity was because the concert had sucked everybody over there.

"Walking toward the music" isn't a bad philosophy of life. Doors might seem closed, the evening might seem prematurely over, but if you can catch a glimpse of nightlife or the sound of music in the distance, why not walk toward it and see what you find?

Some Christians find themselves in a dating dead end. There's no one suitable where they work or at their church. For their own reasons, they refuse to look at any online dating options. Instead of putting themselves in social environments where they might find someone, they start to feel bitter and angry and blame God for not bringing the right one along.

Your passivity is not God's fault. *Walk toward the music.* See what you find. Become proactive, intentional, and even energetic about finding someone to marry. When God, through Scripture, asks young men, "A wife of noble character *who can find*?" (Prov. 31:10), the entire assumption is that such a pursuit involves a serious search.

I asked people on my Facebook page (www.facebook.com/
authorgarythomas) how they met their spouses and if their meeting
was intentional. There were hundreds of responses, but here are a few,
just to give you some ideas:

Church meetings—such as Bible studies, worship services, small
groups, and singles' events—were the most popular places to meet.

Chrystal, Terrell, Leila, Christina, and a whole bunch of others
met their future spouses via online dating websites, the second most
common answer. Ebony responded to a personal ad.

Friends or relatives (the third most common answer) set many
couples up. One couple met via a company commander in Iraq!
"Walking toward the music" could thus involve actively letting friends
and family members know you'd welcome introductions.

Work was another common place to meet. Melissa was working
at a home improvement store when she noticed a "cute loader." So she
did some background research, found out what he liked, and inte-
grated it into their next conversation.

Meredith saw Patrick on a mission trip, got up the courage to sit
next to him, and took an interest in the music he was listening to. Then
she put her phone number in his phone. It's been there ever since.

Shanice met her husband at an "anti-Valentine's Day" party,
where partygoers weren't allowed to bring a date. She had seen her
future husband on a social media site and made sure her roommate
invited him so she could meet him in person.

Elaine met her eventual husband through mutual comments on
Facebook. Their answers to the same post were intriguing enough that
they decided to meet in person.

Chuck likely has the most creative story ever: his wife was a new
FBI agent, and he was a prosecutor. They met while trying to solve a
kidnapping!

Your passivity is not God's fault.... Become

proactive, intentional, and even energetic

about finding someone to marry.

As you can see, not all of these meetings were intentional. But the variety demonstrates how important it is to *keep your eyes open*—at church, school, work, and even online. By all means, keep praying, but also let others know you're interested.

I'm not pretending the search is easy. It's not. In fact, dating can be brutally tough. And I'm not minimizing the experience of so many who write and ask me, "Where are the men and women who want what you talk about in *The Sacred Search*?" There may not be a hundred people that agree with your goals in life and want to marry you, but here's the thing: *you only need one.* You don't have to find a dozen. You don't even have to find two. For a suitable marriage, you just need one.

The message is this: just because it's difficult to find someone, don't go back to your hotel room and call it a night. Walk toward the music. Make the effort. It's worth it.

Make an Investment

Waiting for someone to "find" you is like hoping to get rich by playing the lottery. The opposite and wiser approach is to make many sound investments. Instead of waiting around and hoping you get lucky in love, then, focus on making regular wise investments.

- *Resolve to be even more intentional.*

Tell friends what you're looking for. Be strategic about where you recreate, work, shop, and worship. Get up and take action instead of crossing your fingers and waiting. That's what God specifically tells us to do in Proverbs 31:10. It's even what Abraham sent his servant to do on behalf of Isaac.

- *Increase your odds of marrying well by focusing on your own character—spiritually, financially, relationally, and emotionally—so that you become more attractive as a marriage partner.*

No one "owes" it to you to marry you. And you wouldn't want someone to marry you because that person feels sorry for you, so focus on building your character. Learn how to hold your own in a conversation. Don't go heavily into debt. If you need to get in shape, do so. "Waiting on God" can be a cop-out if you're not working on yourself. Maybe God's waiting on you to get your house in order.

- *Laziness and fear never honor God.*

The Bible is brutal when denouncing sloth and fear. God honors action and courage.

- *While pursuing marriage is a good and holy pursuit, it shouldn't become your primary pursuit.*

We are told to seek *first* the kingdom of God and His righteousness, not seek first marriage. So don't put your faith, worship, and service on a shelf, assuming you can pick it back up once you find your mate. Get involved in God's work. Read books on spiritual growth, and engage in small groups that challenge and inspire you.

Instead of playing the lottery and hoping you get lucky, make many small investments. There's no guarantee, but even if you don't find someone to marry, you'll come out a stronger and better person as you wait, and that's certainly worthwhile on its own.

I truly hope this chapter doesn't come off sounding harsh or as if I'm blaming you. I feel for your desire to be married; it's a holy and good desire, and I know many are wounded in their frustration of romantic relationships that never seem to work out (or that never even start). It's not always easy to find someone to marry, but a good marriage is worth the effort. Take a break when you need to, but after you recover, jump right back in, eagerly and prayerfully, knowing that God is with you in this pursuit.

Searching Questions

1. Think about when you have ever believed the open-
    ing statement of this chapter: "When it comes to
    choosing a mate, God will bring the right person to
    me at the right time. I'll just sit back and wait." After
    reading this chapter, have your thoughts changed
    at all?
2. In what ways can you begin walking toward the
    music?
3. Since studies show most people eventually find
    their mates at church or work or are introduced
    through family and friends, what can you do in the
    coming months to more earnestly pursue a mar-
    riage partner through these avenues?
4. What things might you need to address or improve
    in your own life in order to be more attractive as a
    marriage partner?

Better to Marry Than Burn

I asked a young woman at my church who works with the twenty-something female members of our congregation: how many disciples of Christ—not just women, but those who are sincerely following the Lord—consistently fall in regard to premarital sex?

Without hesitation she responded, "At least 70 percent."

Some of these, she said, feel tremendous guilt every time they fall. Others have rationalized that since so many other Christians are doing it, it must not be wrong, that "saving sex for marriage" must be an outdated religious rule the church needs to grow out of.

One contributing issue that doesn't get addressed enough in this regard is the delay of marriage. For much of human history, people routinely got married in their midteens. In the United States during the 1950s, 1960s, and 1970s the average age of a woman getting married was around twenty. In 2020 it was close to twenty-eight.

This is a tricky situation because the divorce statistics for those who marry young (prior to twenty-five) are significantly higher than those who wait a little longer to get married. That's why some counsel that singles should wait until their late twenties or early thirties.

Delaying marriage does, however, open the door to increased sexual temptation for men and women. For singles who want to honor God in their pursuit of marriage, here are a few things to consider:

- God designed most of us to get married. A few may be called to celibacy, but statistician Dr. Nathan Yau has found that over 90 percent of us will experience marriage at least once in our lives.
- You'll never have a larger pool to draw from for a suitable, godly marriage partner than during your university years or if you attend a large church with an active singles group.
- God made you a sexual being but commands you to restrict sexual activity to marriage (1 Cor. 6:15–20; 7:36–38; 1 Thess. 4:3–7). For some of you it will become overwhelmingly difficult, to the point of courting temptation, to delay the marriage that will allow a holy expression of sexual activity.

According to US census data, the average age for a man or woman to get married in this country is increasing (in 2019 for men it was 29.8 and for women, 28). In spite of this, the fact is, God created you with a body that is ready for sexual activity a decade before that. I don't believe most eighteen-year-olds are ready for marriage—but hang with me here. I don't pretend to have all the answers for how Christians can navigate this divide between sexual interest and delayed marriage. I'm not suggesting we start encouraging everyone to get married before turning twenty-five just to avoid premarital sex. Early marriage may not be the answer in every case, but sexual predation and widespread shame aren't either. Is it wise to not even take this divide into account when so many seem so unable to resist the allure?

Sexual Desire: A Motivation to Marry?

Few people today would question the motivation of a young couple who proclaimed, "We want to get married because we are head over heels in love," even though what they are experiencing is a flood of neuropeptides that neurologists tell us will not and cannot last longer than twelve to eighteen months. On the other hand, sexual need and desire will be a constant for at least the next four or five decades, if not more. Why is it nobler to base a lifelong decision on a relatively temporary emotional disposition and disregard a God-designed motivation that may never fade? Not *once* does the Bible say, "If you're out of your mind with infatuation, by all means, get married!" But it *does* say, "It is better to marry than to burn with passion [or sexual desire]" (1 Cor. 7:9 NASB).

We Christians—believing in God as Creator—should be the *last* ones to discount the delight and pleasure of sexuality *or* the need to respect God's design for this relationship to take place within a lifelong commitment. In fact, marriage is God's creation, and we should surrender to it as part of our worship. If sexual temptation isn't an issue in your life, these words don't apply to you. But if you are trapped in a continuous cycle of disobedience that brings constant shame and regret and even seems to be erecting a wall between you and God, the apostle Paul offers an intentional pursuit of marriage as a "biblical" solution.

Cultural Conditioning

Those of you struggling with sexual temptation but still insisting on a romantic "storm of emotion" before marrying should at least realize the cultural conditioning at work.

Dr. Hsu, a Chinese anthropologist, wrote, "An American asks, 'How does my heart feel?' A Chinese asks, 'What will other people say?'" He claimed that "the Western idea of romantic love has virtually no appeal for young adults in China."[1]

A poll of single people in India asked how many would marry a potential partner if he or she had the right traits but the relationship lacked the "emotional chemistry" of infatuation. A full 76 percent said they would marry anyway, while just 14 percent of US students said they would.* A 1988 study found that Indian "arranged" marriages rated higher in marital satisfaction than did American "love" marriages.[2] An Indian woman explained to me, "Love marriages start out white-hot and almost immediately cool down; arranged marriages often start out lukewarm and slowly warm up."

I'm not advocating the process of arranged marriages, but perhaps we can learn from our friends in the East about what provides a better foundation for choosing a long-term marital match. Can we use the wisdom applied in arranged marriages—an objective, practical look at how two people can form a family—while still accepting the reality and thrill of romantic attraction?

To tie this in with the previous section: if you're truly struggling to live an obedient life, perhaps it's time to seek a permanent relationship earlier than you might otherwise. In doing this you might have to "compromise" on feelings of infatuation, but if you can learn to give proper weight to other concerns, that's not such a big risk. It would be foolish, in my opinion, to marry someone of low character just so you could become sexually active within marriage a little sooner. I'm not saying to compromise on that. I am saying that if this is an area where you struggle, it might be a

---

* I realize I cited a similar-sounding study that put the latter number at 9 percent, not 14 percent. Studies differ in their findings, but both studies demonstrate that the number is very low, whether it's 9 percent or 14 percent, or somewhere in between.

good time to double down on an intentional pursuit of finding a suitable person to marry.

By all means, instead of staying at home and wasting time while you complain about how no good men or women can be found, or passing the time on weekends looking for hookups or watching porn, you're much better off putting that time and effort into finding a sole mate with whom you can seek first the kingdom of God.

What about Money Struggles?

One of the most common arguments for delaying marriage is first achieving financial stability. As one who got married at twenty-two, we did indeed marry ourselves into a financial hole that took years to climb out of. On the other hand, getting married seven years sooner than the average man does today, I also enjoyed becoming an adult with the woman I loved (not to mention eighty-four more months of guilt-free, God-honoring sex). And who's to say we wouldn't have struggled financially as singles? Between you and me, I don't see too many uber-wealthy twenty-four-year-old singles who don't have to deposit their paychecks as soon as they receive them. I'd rather face financial privation *with* someone than on my own.

On a cross-country trek with my son and his best friend, my son's friend mentioned that he was afraid getting married too young would cause him to miss out on the "single life." This guy is a committed believer—we had already talked about his desire to remain a virgin until he gets married. So I asked him, "What are you missing out on, exactly? Living with a bunch of guys, watching sports, and maybe drinking beer or playing video games all weekend? Or doing that occasionally but getting to spend every night with a woman you're good friends with, attracted to, and also having an active and satisfying sexual life with?"

If it's about delaying marriage for a year or so to get settled in your job and gain a more solid financial footing, that's one thing. But putting off marriage to indulge adolescent fantasies of eating junk food, watching junk movies, having junk conversations, having junk sex, and drinking junk beer? Sorry, but I just don't see the allure.

On a positive spiritual note—I'm being vulnerable and honest here—by marrying young, I severely curtailed the possibility that my sexual drive might lead me to sin against some of God's daughters. I learned how to use my body to give my wife pleasure and to meet her sexual needs instead of taking advantage of potential girlfriends as I stumbled along, only partially containing my libido. I knew I was vulnerable in that area; I don't have a perfect past. Taking stock of my spiritual weakness, getting married early was a wise thing to do.

For some of you—particularly those of you who are facing the struggles I did—the call to be holy is a veiled call to get *married*. It's better to admit your weaknesses and channel them in a positive direction that God blesses. Caring about not hurting women or tempting men trains you toward compassion. And compassion will serve you very well in marriage. There's no easy answer to this modern dilemma of the increasing gap between sexual interest and the age we marry, but pursuing marriage a little earlier might be a wise move for some.

We Christians—believing in God as Creator— should be the *last* ones to discount the delight and pleasure of sexuality *or* the need to respect God's design for this relationship to take place within a lifelong commitment.

Searching Questions

1. Why do you think the average age of first marriage continues to rise in our culture? Are these good reasons, consistent with Scripture, or do you wish the trend would be reversed?

2. How can someone be motivated by sexual desire but not ruled by it when actively pursuing marriage?

3. How can the church help earnest believers who struggle with great shame because of their weakness in this area?

4. How important is it to you to be "financially secure" before you get married? How can this be balanced against other issues?

5. Were you surprised to learn that arranged marriages often exceed "love marriages" in perceived intimacy in the second decade of marriage? How should this affect the process of choosing to get married in our culture?

9

What's Your Style?

A famous athlete explained that he was divorcing his wife because, "If I wanted a model or television star, I would have married one a long time ago. All I wanted was a housewife."

There's nothing wrong with wanting to marry a woman who has an exciting career and enjoying the extra income that results—or marrying a woman who wants to focus on the home and be a full-time mom and wife. The problem is that couples often aren't honest about what they want *before* they get married, which leads to great conflict (and sadly, divorce) after marriage.

When it comes to this issue, don't ask yourself what's politically correct to desire or what you *should* desire. Be honest: What do you really want? Be careful about compromising on it because if you make an exception, a small regret can grow into a great frustration that leads to divorce.

"Seeking first the kingdom of God" is a very wide umbrella. There are different ways of seeking that kingdom and expressing God's righteousness. You can be businesspeople or missionaries, you can live focused on the arts or athletics or media. Your goal is to bring the light and truth of Christ into whatever sphere God places you. The kingdom becomes more important than your own agenda, reputation, comfort, or financial gain. The sports broadcaster or veterinarian is no more or less called to seek first the kingdom of God than a nurse or pastor.

The challenge, when applying this to marriage, is getting two people together who agree on the same path. Don't assume that you and a potential partner's motivations are the same or that you even mean the same thing when you say "married." There are many different styles of marriages, and too few singles ever explore this disconnect.

As you embark on your search for a sole mate, ask yourself what your ideal marriage will look like. Will the two of you spend your lives "sucking the marrow out of life" or working hard to establish a business and/or ministry (and often spending evenings and weekends recovering)? Will you seek to build a child-centered family, focusing on the kids, or have you always thought you'd like to do a lot of foreign travel or maybe adopt one or two children? Will you have separate hobbies, or would you prefer to do everything together?

Many people assume their partners are looking for the same things they are when they talk about "being married," but that is rarely the case. We have an image in our minds of what our marriage will be like, but we don't usually label it or even express it. We just assume that our partners share it.

Two people who are both hungry don't necessarily want to eat at the same restaurant; two people who want to get married are not necessarily seeking the same style of relationship. In fact, many people often aren't aware of what they want. They have unspoken, unnamed assumptions. Until you see marriage patterns listed, your wants may not occur to you.

Once you become serious about someone to marry, you and your potential spouse need to get vulnerable and be as honest as you can. The temptation will be to say what you think the other person wants to hear, but that's setting up both of you for considerable disappointment and even lifelong frustration. *Lying about what you want out of marriage because you're afraid you'll lose the relationship if you're honest is one of the worst kinds of fraud you could ever commit.*

You're asking someone to give his or her life over to a lie. And you'll eventually be found out. You can't sustain a lie for fifty years. You may worry about hurting someone's feelings if you begin to sense that the two of you aren't compatible, but be more concerned about hurting that person's life.

To give you a practical tool to help you do this, we're going to look at some of the more common marriage "styles."[1] Some of these are terrible reasons to get married, while others are morally neutral—preference more than values. You shouldn't get too serious with someone until you've carefully considered your own motivations and future desires and then gained a decent understanding of what your partner is looking for.

We all have a mixture of motivations, but this tool will help you understand your unspoken assumptions. If you allow yourself the freedom that comes from the truth that there isn't just one person you can marry, you'll be more objective and honest when going through this exercise.

Rank your desire for each of the following styles of marriage on a scale of 1 to 10 (1 = this isn't me at all and it would be difficult for me to be married to a person who wants a marriage like this; 10 = this describes my assumed view of the marriage relationship very accurately). The best way to be objective here is to rank yourself independently of your partner (or, for many of you, take this test before you even get a partner).

A Spiritual Sole Mate

This person is passionately committed to getting married for the glory of God first and foremost. Such people want to build families that will model God's ministry of reconciliation to the world. They want to raise kids who will follow and serve God. They want to create homes that are a fortress for God's work on this earth. They want to partner with someone who will help them grow to become ever more like Christ.

Seeking a spiritual sole mate above all else doesn't mean you don't have *other* motivations and additional marital styles, however. I'm hoping that the spiritual sole mate model will rule every Christian's heart and that these other styles will be subsets, but I'm also realistic that spiritual maturity is something we grow into and that maturity brings evolving motivations.

If you're already in a serious relationship, try to be honest and ask, Would my partner truly pursue a "spiritual sole mate" marriage, or does he or she just want to be married to me and know I wouldn't have it any other way? And then ask yourself, Is the spiritual sole mate model of marriage something I'm willing to compromise on, something I feel only mildly interested in, or something I am passionately committed to?

I can't tell you how many discouraged women have come to me because they compromised and married spiritually anemic men. They thought that everything else going well in the relationship would make up for a lack of spiritual fervor. To a woman, every one I've talked with has regretted making this compromise. If you want a spiritually rich marriage, you must marry a spiritually alive (and growing) man or woman.

Your rank: _____

Business Buddies and Romantic Idealists

After Prince Charles and the future Princess Diana announced their engagement, an interviewer asked Prince Charles if the couple was "in love." Diana jumped in and answered for her future husband by saying, "Of course." Obviously flustered and taken aback, Charles added a famous addendum: "Whatever 'in love' means." It was a painful moment, and one that proved prophetic. In hindsight, they were seeking two very different things in their relationship. Charles seemed to be seeking a good match for a future king; Diana appeared to be seeking romance, fulfillment, and a storybook life.

Some people, like Charles, are looking for a life partner who is a "good fit." Together they can build a business, a family, a church, a name, or even rule a nation. They are not carried away by romantic notions or expectations; all that seems rather silly to them. They want a suitable partner for a satisfying and productive relationship.

Such a pragmatic matching isn't necessarily a bad thing. Famous director Alfred Hitchcock and his wife, Alma, had a passion to produce iconic movies that strengthened and renewed their passion for each other, leading to a rich partnership and marriage (and work that produced many Academy Award nominations).

But romantic idealists—like Diana—expect to get much of their joy and fulfillment in life from a consistently intimate marriage. They expect their true love to be their best friend and constant lover and to work hard at keeping the romance alive. Romantic idealists can be marked by obsessive clinginess, fear, jealousy, frequent feelings of being slighted, and even acts of desperation. (I don't mean to make this sound unnecessarily negative. It's possible to be a mature and even secure person with a romantic bent; my descriptions, for the sake of clarity, travel to the extremes.) For whatever reason, a romantic idealist's sense of security, self-worth, and happiness are directly tied to the current health, vibrancy, and romantic intensity of the *romantic* relationship. If either partner sacrifices relational time in pursuit of success, hurt feelings will follow.

If you're a romantic idealist, you're going to become very disappointed when your partner focuses on his or her business or hobby. If you're married to a romantic idealist and you're not one yourself, you may become exhausted with the demands placed on you emotionally, physically, and relationally.

What are *your* expectations in this regard? Do you want to join yourself to a suitable partner, or do you want to get lost in a wild, never-ending romance? Without critiquing which you think you should be, admit honestly who you are. (If you think you're in between, you can simply rank yourself a 5 in each category.)

Your rank:

Business Buddy: _____

Romantic Idealist: _____

Adonis and Aphrodite

This is a relationship based on sexual attraction and beauty. In its crassest form, it's when you see the bodybuilder marry the petite woman who has had various cosmetic enhancements. I'm not trying to suggest that every such coupling is so superficial—many times it may not be—but it helps to point out a potentially troublesome motivation. While physical attraction is a key component for marital satisfaction, if it becomes the *main* attraction, what are you going to do when your body ages?

To be fair, sometimes such attractions are due to lifestyle more than appearance. Healthy living, healthy eating, and fitness are noble values. If physical attraction is the main thing drawing the two of you together—even if it's through things like exercise and competition—what happens if your health-loving spouse gets cancer or suffers a stroke? Mutual attraction is a shaky foundation because marriage is about growing old together more than it is about being young together.

Is this a person for whom age will *increase* your devotion and respect, or will this person gradually lose what most draws you to him or her now? Are you in this relationship because the sexual chemistry and attraction is so strong or because the respect and honor you feel for this person is so deep? Beauty and strength serve a ten-year Hollywood career very well, but they're painfully short-lived servants of a fifty-year relationship.

Your rank: _____

Cookbook Couple

A "cookbook" relationship exists when one partner thinks all that's needed is to just find the right strategies, add in the correct ingredients, and then this person gets just what he or she wants out of the relationship. Such people typically read a lot of how-to books, fill out several relationship surveys, and want many sessions of relationship-oriented discussion.

I'm not suggesting that advice books aren't helpful, but if you're going to marry a cookbook spouse, you'd better be ready to participate in these kinds of discussions. This type of spouse is going to want to be in marital counseling (which is a *good* thing; every couple could benefit from counseling now and then), reserve some weekends for marriage conferences, and give you books and articles that he or she will want you to read—and be very frustrated if you don't. Many positive things come about from being married to someone who wants to continually improve skills as a communicator and spouse, but some people would see such a relationship as exhausting. If a cookbook partner is marrying someone who despises that approach, the couple will feel great frustration. If they both enjoy that sort of thing, their common bent will help them build deep intimacy rather than threaten it. They may, indeed, end up with an all-star marriage.

Your rank: _____

The Passionate Partnership

A passionate partnership is marked by two people who are committed to making each other the highest priority—above recreation, child-rearing, vocation, extended family, hobbies, and just about anything else (notice I didn't say "God"). A passionate partnership can seem intimately intense and satisfying when two people enjoy it and suffocating when just one of them wants it.

A person with a passionate partnership mentality reads this and thinks, "Of course, doesn't everybody want this?"—not realizing she may be dating someone who really enjoys focusing on his business but doesn't want to talk about it when he comes home. Or a guy marries a woman who is so into her kids and homeschooling that she would perhaps rather her husband take the kids out for a nature walk when he gets home from work than spend forty-five minutes reliving his day with her. Some guys would rather play eighteen holes of golf on Saturday morning *without* their wives. Other couples think any hobby in which both can't participate is simply unacceptable.

Ideally, every marriage should prioritize the marital relationship above work and even parenting—but passionate partners take it a notch higher. Whatever they experience, they want to experience together, so if one is called away on a business trip, the other will try to come along. Long conversations, plenty of time alone as a couple, and making each other the emotional center of their existence are expected, enjoyed, and cherished.

Two people sharing this vision will, indeed, maintain an intensely intimate and satisfying relationship. They will not have problems with leaving the kids for a date night or a weekend away; indeed, both will be committed to this and even look forward to it. They may well look forward to becoming empty nesters so that they can once again focus on each other. The problem arises only when you have one who wants to have a passionate partner relationship and one who doesn't.

Your rank: _____

The Horror-Show House

This is a relationship style that has no upside, and I mention it so you can avoid it. Some people become interested in a relationship only when they are terrorized by or terrorizing their partner. It's true. These couples fight, argue, make each other miserable and afraid, and may even have quite vigorous makeup sex. Exhausted and spent, they peacefully coexist for another short season until routine sets in and they start the horror cycle all over again.

The problems with such a relationship are many. Often, the one who once felt comfortable being terrorized eventually gets tired of it. And this form of love is so directly in opposition to agape biblical love and marriage that it's a relationship doomed to fail.

If you feel most connected to someone when he is terrorizing you, or you feel closest to someone when you are terrorizing her, you need to know this is a spiritual sickness and a fake intimacy. You need to get healed, not married, *and in that order.* You can't build a healthy relationship on an unhealthy pattern of relating. You need to deal with this before you even think about making a lifelong choice. Not only is it personally destructive, it's a prescription for parental disaster. Kids crave stability and are harmed significantly by never-ending crises.

Your rank: _____

House and Home Marriage

We lived by a neighbor who was obsessed with her yard. She mowed the lawn every other day. Just about every other week she was spreading some new fertilizer or growth aid on the grass. Every time she spoke with us, she talked about her plants, her edging, her landscaping, and the health of her trees as if they were her children.

Other people fixate on a home's interior. If you added up how much time they spent on the internet checking out new furniture, fixtures, home accessories, and the like, it would put their Bible study to shame. Remodeling is to them a fulfilling hobby, and they will never truly be done tinkering with their house or yard.

Others see the house as a place to retreat to and may even enjoy living in an aesthetically pleasing house, but they certainly don't want to sacrifice several weekday evenings and Saturday or Sunday afternoons to keep it up. They'd rather exercise, go to a movie, take a walk, or even take a nap.

This is largely a matter of choice, but when it becomes a problem is if one partner is more concerned about hospitality than house projects or if one would rather spend three thousand dollars on a trip to Europe than on a new sofa. You're also going to run into problems if one would rather get more aggressive in his or her financial giving than spend the money on lawn equipment or plants.

Be honest. How will you focus your energies: on a mansion or a mission? If you're a mission person marrying a mansion person, you're going to be very frustrated.

Your rank: _____

The Kids Are Us Couple

Kids Are Us couples can't wait to have children—sometimes lots of children—and have a relationship that is often focused on the children. They may have occasional date nights, but even this might be done with a view toward modeling a good marriage—*for the children*. Homeschooling or expensive private schooling may often be a priority. This means an extra part of the budget, space in the house, and time on the clock are spent focusing on the kids. Even vacations may be chosen with educational or family fun in mind.

You can love and enjoy kids without being a Kids Are Us couple. But if you are truly a Kids Are Us man who marries a woman who wants, at most, two children, and can't wait until they enter preschool at age three, you will be sorely tried and deeply disappointed with your life. If you're a woman who dreams of having three natural-born children and adopting another three or four and you're marrying a man who might, at most, be willing to put up with two of his own biological children, you're making a big mistake.

Your rank: _____

Bohemian Buddies

Do you envision Sunday mornings or early afternoons taken up with reading through the *New York Times*, checking out the latest indie movie, having a home full of books, going to concerts, regular foreign travel, and fulfilling (as opposed to lucrative) vocations? That's fine, unless you marry a person who is dedicated to business or devoted to ministry to the down-and-out or centered around the life of the local church. This is also one of those lifestyles that usually precludes having lots of kids. It's one thing to raise ten kids on a farm or five kids in the suburbs, but it's a little more difficult to have a large family while living in Manhattan or downtown Seattle.

If you truly aspire toward an arts-oriented lifestyle, you'll be frustrated hanging around with a partner who puts mass-produced prints on the walls and listens to exclusively mainstream music. And this is one preference that really is difficult to compromise on. A woman can join a book discussion group if her husband doesn't read, but what about vacations? What about weekends and evenings? If he just wants to read the *Wall Street Journal* and listen to Fox News or CNN while she was hoping to check out a movie or browse a used bookstore, neither partner is going to feel much rest or intimacy on any given weekend or evening.

A quick warning here: I'm throwing around a lot of stereotypes. It's certainly possible for someone to read the *Wall Street Journal* and still be into the arts. This is intended to start a discussion. The main point is to encourage you to consider who you really are rather than base your marriage on an ideal view of yourself that doesn't square with reality. It's also designed to help you push past the blindness inherent in infatuation so that you can objectively evaluate whether someone you're crazy about is a good fit.

Think about your passions here, and write the appropriate number in the blank below.

Your rank: _____

Police Partners

Some people find themselves energized by a police arrangement—either they want to have somebody they can keep checking up on, or they need somebody to keep checking up on them. If one spouse is or was an addict, the other spouse will regularly check the garbage for bottles, the internet history for sites visited, the bank statements for unexplained withdrawals.

Some people feel most comfortable fulfilling the role of a traffic cop, as it preoccupies their attention and keeps them from having to think about their own shortcomings. It gives them a sense of purpose, and sometimes even feeling fear and suspicion is more energizing than feeling bored or apathetic.

Other people like to be policed; it absolves them from having to look after themselves. They'll keep running into trouble because their partner acts like a safety net, ready to catch them so they don't hit the ground too hard. They may act like they resent the interference, but deep down, they know they need it.

There are considerable problems with entering this kind of marriage. First, if you're the "police," you're assuming you don't need someone to hold *you* accountable. If you're the criminal or in the "save me" role, you're indulging your laziness by refusing to love, look after, or serve someone else. That makes this relationship character-corrupting rather than character-forming.

There can be a sense of satisfaction in thinking you're the only one who really understands her or you're the one he desperately needs because it can feel good to be needed. There's nothing wrong with wanting to help someone out; there is something wrong with choosing an untrustworthy, crisis-prone person to become your spouse. When it comes to choosing a marriage partner, avoid the messianic complex. There is only one Savior, and it's not you.

We'll touch on this more later: Do you really want to raise kids with someone who needs to be rescued from himself or herself? Is that truly the kind of father or mother you want to give your children?

One engaged man admitted he was already "exhausted" with his fiancée's clinical mood swings. If he's exhausted *now*, in a dating relationship, how tired do you think he's going to be when they have three kids and he has a full-time job? Plenty of other men could handle this without being depleted by it. Be honest about what you're capable of handling for the rest of your life.

Your rank: _____

Warriors

Some people like to argue. Maybe it's what they grew up with; it's how they process emotions; it's what keeps life from being so boring. And they may even think that makeup sex is the best kind of sex.

Fighting releases adrenaline, which can make us feel more fully alive. But it's a destructive way to stave off boredom, and it's a disastrous living arrangement in which to raise children. If you can't express what you really feel about each other without using four-letter words and hurtful comments, you lack the basic relational skills necessary to build a satisfying marriage. Either you're not ready for marriage, or the person you're with isn't capable of having an intimate marriage.

There will be seasons of life when you need encouragement, forgiveness, and acceptance; a marriage style defined by fighting usually lacks these essential qualities. Conflict is an inevitable and necessary part of every healthy, mature relationship, but I wouldn't want to be married to someone who is *energized* by altercations. I'd rather my spouse be energized by service, motivated by love, and moved by compassion, kindness, and God's gentle leading.

Your rank: _____

Student-Teacher

One person likes to learn; one likes to teach. The most common form is the much older, usually financially successful man or woman marrying a considerably younger spouse. He thinks it's "cute" that she is enthralled by fancy restaurants she's never been to before, and when he explains the wine list to her and she looks at him with awe, it makes him feel like a *man*.

Women can get an ego rush having a younger man chase after them, and for a while they may enjoy doing "younger" things, reliving an earlier life. But if that's the main attraction in your marriage, how long can you sustain that kind of bond? Your "young" man won't be so young in another decade.

There can also be a "spiritual" parent-teacher relationship—the mature believer leading an unbeliever to the Lord and being his or her primary spiritual influence.

The most solid marriages are mutual—where each partner contributes to and challenges each other and the "power balance" shifts rather than centers on one or the other. Students eventually grow up and want to be in a more mature relationship. Being a student is okay for a while, but eventually you want to graduate. If the person you're married to won't let you do that, resentment is inevitable. You want to kill a sexual relationship? Sow the seeds of resentment. It works every time.

These are short-term situations at best and usually don't make a healthy basis for a long-term marriage.

Your rank: _____

Finding Your Match

Perhaps I've yet to describe your ideal marriage style. That's okay; I'm just trying to get the conversation going. Jennifer liked to go out several times a week; she was a social butterfly. Her husband, Riley, developed properties for contractors and worked long days. The hard labor made him want to plop on the couch as soon as he got home. When Jennifer mentioned a party or friends getting together at a restaurant, Riley felt that taking a shower and heading back out was the last thing he wanted to do.

Neither Jennifer nor Riley were right or wrong in their evening preference. Working hard was what Riley did. Needing to enjoy a good dinner party on a regular basis was part of Jennifer's DNA. Jennifer and Riley eventually got divorced. I'm not saying their dramatically different social preferences were the main cause, but they certainly didn't help. This is something I wish they would have considered *before* they got married.

You shouldn't get too serious with someone until you've carefully considered your own motivations and future desires and then gained a decent understanding of what your partner is looking for.

Take the time to write out a description of your ideal marriage style. It might not be one that I mentioned above. Describe with *detailed* scenarios what sounds most exciting and rewarding to you.

- How will you spend your evenings?
- How close will the two of you be?
- Will you try to spend every hour outside of work together, or will you sometimes pursue separate hobbies and ministry opportunities?
- How central will church involvement be in your life?
- Will you take vacations with the kids, without the kids, or even perhaps individually?
- When you've daydreamed about the most satisfying moments of marriage, are you and your loved one walking on a beach, scouring antique stores, working on a mission field, taking your children to the park, or doing something else?

If you're already in a dating relationship, compare your answers, and then bring them up in a group setting. This group step is important because sometimes men and women are more likely to be honest when they see others sharing their views. Guys might be shy telling their girlfriend, "Yeah, I'm not so into the handyman thing," but when *another* guy says it first, your guy can laugh and say in a little moment of truth, "You got that right." When a woman says, "You know, I don't really know if I want to have children," your girlfriend's unfiltered facial expression in response will tell you a lot about how she really feels.

Labels aren't nearly as important as how well your assumptions about married life match up with those of the person you're thinking about marrying. If your partner is antagonistic to an activity or style that's important to you, don't try to make yourselves fit into each other's lives; there are other people out there. Remember, if there's not "one right choice," there is likely a more compatible person out there with whom you can share your life in a more fruitful and satisfying manner.

Searching Questions

1. What style of marriage best describes the kind of marriage you've always imagined having?
2. How should a couple respond if the two of them feel deeply in love but recognize that they envisage two very different styles of marriage? How important do you think agreement on marriage styles should be in deciding whom to marry?
3. What differing styles would be most compatible? Which ones would be most toxic if put together?

10

Can You Climb a Mountain Together?

Nobody wakes up one morning and suddenly decides, "I think I'll climb Mount Everest today." Such a monumental assault requires training, preparation, and physical gear.

Lots of gear.

In fact, experts suggest those who climb Mount Everest should approach it with no fewer than *three* separate pairs of boots, plus lots of socks. Tools help keep you alive, so don't scrimp here—you'll want an ice ax, carabiners, ascenders, a rappel device, a climbing harness, trekking poles. To stay warm, you'll need plenty of good underwear, a pile jacket, pile pants, down pants, a down parka, a Gore-Tex shell with a hood, and probably a bib. Along with your sleeping bag you'll need two different sleeping pads (and a repair kit). Plan on two pairs of synthetic gloves and two pairs of pile mitts or Gore-Tex over mitts. Hand warmers are optional, but you won't regret bringing them.

Add in months of strength and endurance training and hopefully years of alpine experience at lower altitudes, and it's clear that climbing Everest is a big deal. You need to be prepared.

Just as you wouldn't try to scale a mountain without making sure you have what you need, don't enter the most difficult relationship of your life without someone who has what he or she needs to complete the journey with you. Life is not going to be easy. Prepare for it to be twice as hard as you think it's going to be. If it ends up being easier than you thought, there's nothing lost joining with someone who could have weathered any storm with you. But if you plan for a picnic and marry someone who is only prepared for easy times, then you're going to be in serious trouble if times turn tough.

Some people may want to be married to you, but they may not have what it takes to be part of a successful marriage; the latter is what you need to evaluate and test. Certain relational and life skills are essential to marital happiness and fulfillment. When you're dating, it doesn't take someone of great character to accompany you to movies and nice restaurants, to go on fun bike rides or hikes, or sit in a Starbucks or make out on a couch. Most people can do that.

That's not real life, however—at least, not for very long. As a pastor, I've watched many couples endure excruciating life crises. In this chapter, we'll discuss several essential character traits that aren't at all related to "romantic connection" but that are essential to thrive in a lifelong *marriage*. My goal is to get you to think about a person's potential to climb the mountain of life with you *all the way to the top.*

Some people may want to be married to
you, but they may not have what it takes to
be part of a successful marriage; the latter
is what you need to evaluate and test.

Medical Maelstroms

Ever hear of Angelman syndrome? I've met three families who have given birth to children with this neurogenetic disorder marked by severe intellectual and developmental delays. There is no cure for this malady, meaning today's parents will have to take care of such a child for the rest of their lives.

A high percentage of marriages with severely disabled children end in divorce. Caring for a disabled child requires a lot of time, energy, and money. How would the person you're thinking about marrying hold up under the weight of physical exhaustion, spiritual confusion (when God doesn't answer your prayers the way you want Him to), interrupted sleep schedules, neglected hobbies, and old-beater cars to pay for extra medical care? Is he or she the kind of person who can still find joy in marriage in the face of such challenges?

Darell wore a big tux when he got married, not because he was overweight but because he was a bodybuilder who could benchpress four hundred pounds. You don't fit pecs like that into a 38R coat. His wife, Stacey, was attracted to his physique and admired his strength. She valued being married to a physically fit man.

Just two years into their marriage, however, Darell started experiencing some concerning symptoms: numbness, vision loss, and tremors. Medical tests revealed heartbreaking news: Darell had multiple sclerosis. Stacey's strong, athletic husband bravely fought off going into a scooter for as long as possible, but his legs couldn't carry him much past his forty-fifth birthday. That leaves a lot of life, a lot of marriage, to be lived. For most of their days together, even though Stacey married a strong, bodybuilding husband, she's had to do most of the heavy lifting.

Jake married an accomplished businesswoman, Grace, who worked for a prestigious consulting firm. She had the kind of job that sets you up vocationally for life. If you wanted to get an MBA, her firm would get you into Harvard or Wharton. If you wanted to work for a nonprofit or another company, they'd help you do that too. If you wanted to stay with them and slowly grow rich, well, by all means, get to work and prepare to cash the checks.

When Jake and Grace first got married, she earned far more money than he did until an autoimmune disorder began to take over her body and eventually left her bedridden for more than six months. The company was generous—for a while. Finally the company realized Grace wasn't coming back. Jake thought he was marrying a woman who would more than double his income, but now he's married to a woman who will need him to support her, perhaps for the rest of her life.

You don't know what the future holds, but you *can* know the character of the person you decide to marry. Is this person strong enough to take a similar hit and keep going? The spiritual ability to maintain hope even in the face of pressure-packed obstacles is an essential quality in life. "Against all hope, Abraham in hope believed" (Rom. 4:18). Don't minimize the importance of marrying someone who is spiritually tough, who doesn't grumble, and who doesn't turn against God at the first sign of trouble. Life is usually full of trouble.

Your Kids' Parent

During an interview, a Hollywood actress didn't rave to the reporter about her husband's wealth, celebrated looks, or reputation. Instead, watching her husband on set with one of their children, she said, "The one thing I can say I did a good job on, I found a great man to father kids with. It's like if I didn't do anything else right in this world, my kids got a good doggone daddy."[1]

For many of you, discussions of future children are all theoretical. When kids are actually born and have names and you can touch them and look into their adorable eyes, you will experience emotions and a capacity for sacrificial love you never even knew existed. You would be willing to swim across the ocean in a lead coat in order to save them. The most significant act of love, however, takes place before they're born. Before you agree to marry anyone, ask yourself, Would this be the best mother/father for my children? The time will come when, like this actress, you will be more grateful than you can imagine—or more regretful than you've ever been—because you have chosen for them a wonderful or abusive parent.

This wasn't at the top of the list when I was thinking about the woman I should marry, but I did think Lisa would turn out to be a devoted mom—and was I right. She was a creative homeschool teacher until our kids reached high school; their subsequent educational career paths benefitted enormously from her sacrifice and service.

I also remember the funeral of a friend's mom. She was a quiet woman, but the kind of mom who, according to my friend, "let the house be messy so she could sit down and talk with us." The family wasn't high achieving, but they experienced much warmth, happy memories, and raucous celebrations.

You get to choose what kind of parenting style you want to bring into your own family: scholastic, fun times, low pressure, high achieving, devout, neglectful—and the person you choose to marry will have a major impact on that goal.

Most importantly, I hope you'll want your children to share your faith. Is the person you're planning to marry the kind of man or woman who will help this happen or hinder it?

A young woman who self-described as a "seriously committed" Christian was planning to marry an agnostic man whose parents were Buddhists. She asked me what I thought.

"Do you want your future children to become Christians?"

"More than anything," she replied.

"Then let me paint you a scenario. Your husband never goes with you to church, but you take your boy every week because you want more than anything for him to embrace Jesus as his Savior and Lord. When that boy turns eight, he asks his father, 'Dad, why don't you come to church with us?' and Dad answers, 'Son, I don't believe that stuff and here's why.'"

Pausing, I asked her, "Do you think hearing a dad he idolizes dismiss your faith is something that will help him grow toward God or get in the way? And when he spends the night at Grandpa and Grandma's house and sees their Buddhist shrine and hears them talk about their faith, you've got a kid who sees one parent go to a Christian church, one parent dismiss faith altogether, and grand-parents who practice an entirely different religion. If you want your future kids to become Christians 'more than anything,' is this the kind of environment you'd choose for your son?"

In addition to wanting your kids to know the one true God, you're also going to want them to be loved by *both* parents. Not tolerated, not merely provided for, but engaged with, loved, and cherished.

You're not just choosing a life partner. You're choosing your kids' future mom or dad. Is this person worthy of that job?

Single parents usually *do* think about the kind of parent they'd be choosing, often making it one of the top criteria before entering a dating relationship. Those without children would do well to follow their lead.

Your Kids' Grandparents

This one is not nearly as absolute as the previous category. It's a nice addition, but I wouldn't by any means call it a deal breaker. Still, it's worth considering that you're not just choosing your kids' future *parent*; you're choosing your kids' future *grandparents*. If you want to build a family of faith, it's helpful to have a legacy to build on. You'll appreciate having another couple who will actively pray for your child and who will speak and act in such a way that affirms what you're trying to do at home (this is *especially* the case if your own parents are whacked-out). Your kids will see their grandparents share your faith, treat each other a certain way, and talk about others a certain way. That creates stability and gives them that much more of a foundation from which their own faith can be conceived and nurtured.

In his book *Stepping Up*, Dennis Rainey tells the tear-drenched story of how his daughter Rebecca and her husband, Jake, gave birth to a little baby whose brain was almost gone by the time she was born. Little Molly lived just seven days, but in that one love-packed week, she received abundant care, prayers, and comfort. Because both Rebecca and Jake come from strong families, *two* sets of grandparents were there, praying over little Molly, reading Scripture to her, and singing songs of worship along with her parents. Here's how Dennis describes Molly's final moments on earth, when they all knew she was about to die and planned their last good-byes:

> Barbara was first. It was quite a maneuver to make sure all the wires and tubes that were supporting Molly's life didn't get tangled, but finally there she was in her arms. Barbara kept saying how much of an honor it was to hold this little princess of the King. She held her close and cooed words of love

and admiration over her beautiful face. Holding back tears was impossible.

When it was Bill's turn, he stroked her face, tenderly whispered his love for her, and shared his favorite scriptures with her. Pam beamed as she gently rocked Molly and sang "Jesus Loves Me" to her. Both Bill and Pam just held her, kissing her face, holding her little hands, and weeping as they said good-bye.

As Molly was placed in my arms, she felt so warm, just like every newborn. I tried to sing to her, and I doubt that she recognized "Jesus Loves Me" as I choked out a few words through tears.[2]

As his own kids were growing up, Dennis used to tell stories of a fantasyland filled with "Speck people." Dennis always got one of the Speck people into a harrowing dilemma and then said, "And you'll have to wait until tomorrow night to hear the rest of the story." He then frequently told these stories to his grandchildren, so Jake asked his father-in-law, Molly's grandfather, to tell her one Speck story before she died.

At first, Dennis protested—he just couldn't. But Jake and Rebecca implored him, which led to this:

> I held little Molly, looked into her face, and began my story: "A Speck grandfather and his Speck granddaughter went fishing for tiny Speck fish…."
> My story was less than sixty seconds long, and when I looked up into Rebecca's face, she had the biggest grin, dimples and all. She was loving the moment.

As I concluded my story, I told Molly, "The Speck grandfather and granddaughter took their fish and ate them, and then they encountered something you would never expect or believe ... and you will have to wait until I get to heaven to hear the rest of the story."

At this point I was sobbing, but I got the words out ... and Rebecca and Jake started laughing. Rebecca's laughter has always been contagious, and I, too, began to really laugh.[3]

Losing a child is one of the most painful experiences any human can ever know. But the corporate love of four faith-filled grandparents allowed this young mom and dad to find *laughter* and *hope* in the face of one of life's ugliest realities.

It gets even better: with all the laughter in the room, little Molly's oxygen monitor, which had been at an anemic 80 percent, shot up to 92 percent, then 94, 97, 98, 99, and then, finally, 100. That tiny newborn drank in the faith and hope and laughter of her parents and grandparents. Though this was ultimately her last day on earth, I don't doubt that she died knowing she was very loved, and she is no doubt eagerly waiting in heaven to greet first her grandparents and then her parents, who gave her such a sweet and blessed passing.

You have a chance—one opportunity—to choose such a legacy for yourself and for your children.

That's the positive view. On the negative end, if your boyfriend's or girlfriend's prior generations contain dangerous issues, be very cautious. Child abuse, sexual deviancy, psychological problems, and addictions not only will make your potential spouse

more vulnerable as he or she ages (some of these problems sometimes take a while to sprout) but can also be passed down, in some
sense, to your kids. I'm not saying it's always direct, but the statisti-
cal evidence is concerning.

A friend who went through a heartbreaking divorce confessed:
"What I didn't know when I met or married this guy was that there
was a family history of mental illness. You just don't think to ask,
'So, has anyone in your family ever had a lobotomy? Really? Two
of your uncles? And one nearly killed his wife and kids?? Really??'
There are mentally ill people, male and female, who are capable of
becoming or saying or doing anything they think will help them
accomplish a goal. This guy I married was physically and sexually abusive.... He was a Jekyll/Hyde, a liar/deceiver, and I didn't
recognize the wolf in sheep's clothing."

She would be the first to tell you to thoroughly do your
homework in checking out any delicate issues buried in a potential
spouse's family history and not allow the fog of romance to keep
you from doing an extensive family "background check."

Never forget: *you're building a family.* To make a wise investment, you need to consider the other "partners." Is your spouse so
strong in every other area that you're willing to take a risk with
a weak extended family? Or does your potential spouse barely
qualify on his or her own *and* have a nightmare extended family
as well?

I certainly wouldn't urge you to break up with an otherwise
superb mate just because this person comes from a dysfunctional
extended family. I've met many heroic women and men of faith
whose walk with God inspires me and whose character humbles
me, even though their extended families were a mess. But this is
certainly something to explore with your eyes wide open.

Spiritual Maturity

Faith well-lived creates a certain strength that many people admire, even if they don't appreciate where that strength comes from. Because of this, some people who want to marry you may pretend to have strong faith because they know you wouldn't consider them if they didn't. Your job is to figure out if they are into God only because *you're* into God and they're into you, or if your intended is a genuine and passionate follower of Christ without you around.

Consider the following:

Does he or she pray? Not just in church and not just with you, but on his or her own? If not, you'll walk through life without the prayerful support of the person who knows you best. You'll be the only one supporting your kids in prayer. You'll be married to someone who isn't opening himself or herself up to God's conviction, encouragement, and support. If your spouse gets depressed, you'll have to lift this person up on your own, since he or she won't know how to go to God. If you get depressed, you'll have to find another friend to prayerfully support you because your spouse won't know how. If your husband or wife develops bad attitudes toward you or cultivates sinful habits and isn't spending time in prayer to be convicted by God, those attitudes and habits will grow stronger and possibly threaten your marriage.

At least 90 percent of the changes I've made in my marriage have come through God convicting me in prayer and Bible study rather than Lisa confronting me. If I didn't pray very often, Lisa would be a much less satisfied spouse. If you marry someone who prays, you can place your hope in God's *conviction* instead of your *nagging* (which never works).

A woman once told me that she feels so much safer when she knows her husband is praying and in the Word. She doesn't have to ask him if he's doing this—she can tell by his attitude, his actions, the tone of his voice, his overall demeanor. And knowing he is regularly connecting with God gives her a peace and security that she treasures. Notice what she's saying: *the same man* is a different husband when he becomes a praying husband. How do you know if your boyfriend or girlfriend is praying? Ask yourself, does he ever bring up things God is encouraging him with or does she mention what God is challenging her on? Are you always the one mentioning what God is teaching you, convicting you of, or helping you to understand? If your boyfriend or girlfriend never talks *about* God, he or she is probably not talking *to* God.

Is your potential future spouse a student of the Bible? If you marry a man or woman who opens his or her Bible only when the pastor is reading the text, you're marrying someone whose spiritual growth will be negligible and who isn't growing in wisdom. She won't have Scripture on her mind to encourage you or spiritually feed your children. He'll be set in his own prejudices and faulty thinking without being washed by the Word. A spouse like this will never be spiritually wiser than he or she already is.

Finally, **does your intended demonstrate past participation, on his or her own, of being part of a church?** I've seen some couples who agree to go to church while they're dating but then, after marriage, one of them "suddenly" decides to be done with church. In fact, it wasn't sudden at all—the one just *started* going to church to keep the girlfriend or boyfriend's interest. The best way to guard against this is to know that church was a part of your intended's life before he or she met you. Why does going to church matter? A healthy church provides constant instruction, weekly times of renewal with God, and accountability should your spouse start to stray.

We've mentioned some character issues in this chapter; in the next, we're going to talk about some necessary *relationship skills*. Someone could be "strong enough" to be your man or woman but still lack the competence and capability of being an excellent husband or wife when it comes to relational issues.

Searching Questions

1. On a scale of 1 to 10, how difficult do you expect marriage to be? (1 = always easy, if you're truly in love; 10 = a difficult challenge every day)

2. How do you think a person's perception of the difficulty of marriage will influence whom he or she marries?

3. Would you consider marrying someone you felt deeply in love with, even if you didn't think that person was very mature? Where do you draw the line—how mature must someone be (relationally) in order for you to feel comfortable marrying him or her?

4. Have you known any families or couples that had to endure serious medical difficulties? How did that affect their relationship? How did what you observed affect what qualities you expect in the person you're looking to marry?

5. Would you be willing to marry someone who makes you laugh, whose company you enjoy, and whom you are sexually attracted to, even if you're not sure this person would be a good parent? Why or why not?

6. How can you tell ahead of time how good a parent someone might be?

7. Describe the ideal grandparents for your future children. How important does giving your children grandparents like this seem to you?

Making a Marriage

Most Hollywood romances focus on finding "the one." A common plot point is to have two individuals, destined to be together, almost meet. They'll walk right past each other, perhaps even glance and smile as they pass, just seconds apart, as the camera hovers overhead. If only she would walk *that* way, she'd run into him; if only he had turned his head one second sooner … Since the actors are the two best-looking people on the set, you know they will meet eventually, but it creates a little tension to put it off for a while.

This romantic mind-set is based on the false and harmful notion that a good relationship is something you *find*, when in fact it is something you *make*. Infatuation is something you find. Sexual chemistry is something you find. A lost cell phone is something you find. But a strong, intimate, God-honoring marriage that leads to a lifelong partnership and that fosters a sense of oneness? That's something you *make*, and it takes a long time and certain relational skills to achieve.

I want to say this again, because if you'll accept this premise, it'll go a long way toward helping you make a wise marital choice: *a good marriage isn't something you find; it's something you make.*

A relationship requires two people who, even after infatuation and sexual chemistry have faded, continue to keep growing the relationship. Intimacy is created stitch by stitch, through verbal sharing, acts of love and service, expressions of commitment, plenty of forgiveness, and building increased understanding through communicating and experiencing life together.

This chapter builds on the previous one to discuss relational skills that are essential to create and sustain such a thriving marriage. You can't expect a twenty-two-year-old to possess all of them in their full mature form, but you should see the foundations of these elements. The degree to which they are not present is the degree to which you'll have difficulty building intimacy with this person and the degree to which you're going to struggle in the early years of marriage.

A good marriage isn't something you find; it's something you make.

Humility

Humility is not thinking less *of* yourself; it is thinking less *about* yourself. A humble person is someone who, like Jesus, believes he has come "not to be served but to serve" (Mark 10:45 ESV). Jesus knew His talents and He knew His deity, but He used His power to serve. Unlike Jesus (since we are not perfect and He was), humble people have experienced and are experiencing conviction of sin: they are aware that they fall short every day and that they have much to work on, and biblical grace is the only place they put their hope.

The only thing worse than marrying an imperfect person is marrying an imperfect person who thinks he or she is perfect. When you lovingly confront people like this, they'll take offense. Or, horrified that they've been found out, they'll minimize the issue with silly games: "I'm just a horrible, horrible wife." No, you're a good wife who has a sinful issue that needs attention. The reason I call this a game is that unparticular repentance is a clever way to avoid particular conviction. Saying "everything about me is rotten" helps us sidestep the fact that some parts of us are more rotten than others.

While theologically it is true that "all our righteous acts are like filthy rags" (Isa. 64:6), that doesn't mean we don't have some strengths and weaknesses. A wise person knows he or she might excel at giving but lack patience, or excel in patience while lacking courage. The key is to accept that there will always be weaknesses in our lives and, with a spirit of willingness and appreciation, to learn to value a spouse who wants to help us make every effort to add to our faith (see 2 Pet. 1:5–7).

Humility matters more than money and appearance, as it is the character foundation for future growth and godliness. You can always earn more money, lose a little weight, and gain a bit more muscle, but if someone's character has no foundation, there's nothing to build on. Humility is the cornerstone of character and the foundation of a growing, intimate relationship. I don't believe it is possible for a highly arrogant person to be intimately connected with someone. Arrogant people use people; they don't love them. The Bible says no less than three times that God opposes the proud but gives grace to the humble (see Prov. 3:34; James 4:6; 1 Pet. 5:5). Do you want to marry someone who is at war with God or someone who is walking in His grace? A humble person:

- lives with biblical conviction of our overall sin nature as well as particular sins

- lives out the gospel—recognizes that we are help-less to save or even change ourselves, apart from the work of Christ and the empowerment of the Holy Spirit
- is open to receiving appropriate correction and eager to take action when faults are pointed out
- lives authentically—is concerned with growing in righteousness rather than merely appearing righteous
- aspires to excel in being a servant

When she gets into an argument, a humble person considers the fact that she may be wrong and that there may be something she has missed or is overlooking, so she'll spend just as much time trying to understand you as she does presenting her side. A proud person simply wants to convince *you* to change. If, in your disagreements with your boyfriend or girlfriend, the focus is always on what *you* need to do differently without any acknowledgement of what he or she needs to address, you're probably dating a very proud person.

Forgiving

According to the Bible, you are going to stumble many times throughout your marriage (see James 3:2). You will break your spouse's heart. You will disappoint her. You will embarrass him. Your sin will inconvenience her.

A premarital couple I counseled needed to work on building relational intimacy. The guy confessed that he didn't want to fully open up to his fiancée about the stress in his life because he didn't want to be a burden to her. I told him that if his goal is to never be a burden to his future wife, he might as well break up with her right then. There was visible shock on his face until I explained, "What if you get laid off, can't find another job, and she has to double her hours? What if you make a really stupid investment and your retirement portfolio tanks? Over the course of your marriage, you are going to hurt and disappoint this woman very deeply, so you might as well learn how to face it in a way that draws you together instead of pulling you apart."

It's hard to accept that we are going to hurt someone we love so much, but if we marry that person, we will. *That's a biblical promise.* Which means forgiveness is essential. I have seen married couples survive affairs, catastrophic illnesses, financial meltdowns, and tragedies that would make you pass out—but the one thing I have never seen a marriage survive is a persistent unwillingness to forgive.

How do you know the person you love is capable of forgiving? First, that person recognizes his or her own need for forgiveness, understands God's love and acceptance, and not only believes the gospel but has it woven into every fiber of his or her being: we are all sinners saved by grace who depend on God's mercy and initiating grace every hour of our lives.

If your boyfriend or girlfriend is having a difficult time forgiving you for things you've done while dating, marriage is going to be even harder. When you live together and raise a family together, sins become more apparent and more consequential. If that person can't forgive you *now*, he or she will never be able to forgive you *then*.

Forgiveness does not mean the removal of consequences, of course. Women, if your guy cheats on you, you need to forgive him—and most likely, break up with him. If he hits you, even once—you will have to work toward forgiveness, but I pray you will end the dating relationship right then (more on this in a moment) and perhaps even turn him in to the police.

In addressing forgiveness, I'm talking about the kinds of sins that don't speak of a questionable character but rather of a person in progress who needs common grace. Dating is different from marriage; it is appropriate to evaluate your commitment and the person's worthiness as his or her character reveals itself.

Handles Conflict in a Healthy Way

Because both of you stumble in many ways, you need someone who can not only forgive but then work through conflict with you in a healthy way. *There will be conflict.* The question is, How will you respond? Will you grow toward each other, will your hearts grow more distant because you avoid the issue, or will you respond to conflict in hurtful ways?

Any form of violence—threats, yelling, physical violence—is an unhealthy response to conflict. Women, when it comes to physical abuse in dating, my suggested rule is, one strike and he's out. He doesn't get a second chance. If he's a little too angry for you when you're dating, he will become much too angry when you're married. A man who expresses anger with physical violence is on a path toward family destruction. Do you really want to make babies with a guy who will get angry at them and then hit them? Do you want to sleep naked next to a man who might do you bodily harm? Do you want to drive in an SUV with a guy who can't control his temper and may run both of you into a head-on accident (while your children are riding in the backseat)?

Some may accuse me of being unyielding on this, but I believe if a boyfriend hits you, that's all you need to know. He's not the kind of guy you want to marry. Many women have ignored evidence of "a little" violence in a boyfriend and have lived to regret it. That's why I think that if there's *any* violence, you end the relationship right there (and of course this goes for men dating violent women as well). Assume he's on his best behavior while trying to win you over. If he can't keep things under control while you're dating, he'll never be able to handle himself being around you every day.

The best opportunity for an abuser to change would be for him to lose someone he really loves due to his acting out. That might force him to seek help and to learn healthier ways of relating. If you make an exception "just this once," you are training him to expect women "who really love him" to give him a pass when it comes to violence. He needs to understand that physical violence is a completely unacceptable way of solving conflict with those he loves (including his future children).

A woman once told me I'm too black-and-white on this. But if out of romantic silliness you ignore signs of a man's violence, you may one day have to tell your kids, "I'm sorry I chose a dad for you who scares you. I'm sorry you've seen me threatened, maybe even hit. I'm sorry we all feel a little bit safer when your dad is gone and a little nervous whenever he comes home until we find out what kind of mood he's in. However, the infatuation I felt for him was so strong I think, all in all, it's been worth it."

Another form of unhealthy conflict resolution is to talk *about* your partner before you talk *to* your partner. There is nothing wrong with seeking godly input, but complaining about your partner to your friends or family members in a nonredemptive way is called gossip. Dr. Steve Wilke defines gossip as talking negatively about someone to another person who isn't part of the solution. If you haven't talked about an issue with your partner, you have no business talking about it to someone else, unless it's particularly touchy and you're seeking godly wisdom as to how to share it or broach the topic. Talking with others about a conflict should never be a substitute for talking *with* your spouse; it should merely prepare you to talk *to* your spouse.

Healthy conflict resolution, on the other hand, means a person can admit where he or she is wrong. Even if someone is only 10 percent wrong, that person can own the 10 percent. But it is *not* healthy to confess wrongdoing when there is no wrongdoing to confess. Some people will say "sorry" just to bring about peace. That's not healthy, and it's not biblical. You want to find someone humble enough to admit personal failings, wise enough to recognize yours, and courageous enough to hold his or her ground if you are acting arrogantly and refusing to see your sin.

Finally, people who resolve conflict in a healthy way will be willing to seek a third opinion for the times in your marriage when the two of you cannot agree. You may need to find a godly pastor or counselor to hear both of you out and provide wise counsel. I would be hesitant to marry anyone who wouldn't agree to use counseling when necessary, for the simple fact that it *will* be necessary.

Throughout our marriage, Lisa and I have sought counseling for various relationship issues—problems with communicating when the kids were young, issues with parenting as the kids got older (to make sure we were on the same page), and then later in life when we had a series of disappointing setbacks and wanted to learn how to process our grief without growing apart.

In the last round of counseling, a talented counselor helped me to see how much of a codependent I've been my entire life. I had been married thirty-five years without addressing this or even being aware of it, but our marriage has benefited greatly by my finally facing some of my deepest and most buried motivations.

Entering a new marriage is like buying a new car: it runs fine for a while. But eventually that shiny new car is going to need a mechanic. If you're marrying someone who resents mechanics or who is threatened by mechanics, you'd better get used to walking, because your car is going to be broken for a really long time.

Communicates Well

Intimacy is built through sharing, listening, understanding, and talking through issues. If someone doesn't like to talk, refuses to talk, or resents your desire to talk, intimacy building is going to hit a stone wall.

One of the most harmful relational patterns is the silent treatment or what often gets called "stonewalling." When you refuse to talk things out, you're refusing to relate. Ignoring a problem or hurt doesn't make it go away; on the contrary, it enables it and risks adding on bitterness and resentment.

Needing time to process what you're thinking isn't stonewalling, however. Some of us need a little time to figure out how we feel and why we feel that way. As long as you're willing to come back and talk about it, that's a matter of process, not refusal. But statements like "I don't want to talk about it" or "Just forget it and never mention this again" are dangerous markers of stonewalling.

In many (but by no means all) relationships, the woman will desire to talk more than the man, so women shouldn't freak out if their boyfriends don't seem as excited about this aspect of relational building as they are. But, women, if he isn't growing in his desire to share his heart with you, if he is doing it only to please you, if it feels like a chore to him to get to know you, if he can't or won't ask you a question about yourself, then he lacks the basic relational skills to build an intimate marriage. Most women feel cherished and loved when their romantic partner maintains curiosity and interest, and they feel diminished when their romantic partner makes them feel like a bother or an annoyance just because they want to talk.

Skilled in the Art of Friendship

Does your future spouse have friends? Not acquaintances, but true friends? If someone is twenty-eight years old and doesn't have any other close connections, that's a signal that person may not be very skilled at building (or even appreciating) intimate friendships. What makes you think it will be any different with you? At the very least, you need to know you will have to do much of the work to turn this marriage into a friendship and that you're assuming your boyfriend or girlfriend is going to be willing and/or capable of responding in an intimate way. It's always dangerous to assume someone can or will change. Your best bet to make a marriage is to find someone who already knows how to make and keep friends because marriage is the ultimate friendship. Besides, healthy friends outside the marriage feed the marriage in many ways. Asking your spouse to be your *only* friend puts a lot of weight on your relationship.

Making the Call

Okay, now you know some of the basic requirements to build a marriage. If you're in a relationship that appears headed toward marriage, here's a simple test. On a separate piece of paper, assess your potential spouse on a scale of 1 to 10 in each area. This person is:

    ___ likely to be a good parent

    ___ a mature believer

    ___ humble

    ___ forgiving

    ___ healthy conflict resolver

    ___ good communicator

    ___ skilled in the art of friendship

If your total score isn't a fifty-six or higher, I think you need to talk this list through with a pastor, trusted older friend, or counselor to see if the person you're thinking about marrying is going to be capable of building the kind of marriage you desire. If the person you are thinking about marrying lacks the basic skills required to make a marriage, the death of infatuation is going to hit you particularly hard. You won't have a partner who can respond to this necessary life moment by slowly building relational intimacy on a day-by-day basis.

It all comes down to this: if relational intimacy matters to you, make sure you marry someone who has the basic skills to build such a relationship, as well as the motivation to keep on doing so. Once the infatuation ends, relational skills are essential to take your marriage to the next level. This sounds elementary, but it's often ignored in the fog of infatuation.

Searching Questions

1. Do you believe the statement—"A good marriage isn't something you find; it's something you make"—is true? Why or why not?
2. People often consider whether they feel attracted to each other physically while ignoring things like the person's level of humility. How would you balance your value of a person's physical attractiveness with his or her level of spiritual humility?
3. Have you ever asked someone to forgive you? What was that experience like for you? Was the person's reaction similar to what you hope to experience in marriage or something very different?
4. Do you work well through conflict or try to avoid it at all costs? What characteristics should a future mate have for a couple to grow through conflict instead of being crushed by it?
5. Do you agree that any act of violence should end a dating relationship? What boundaries will you set for relational violence so you know when to leave? Have your boundaries ever been crossed?
6. How important do you think regular communication will be for you to fully enjoy your marriage and feel connected to your spouse? How can you tell if someone will communicate after the infatuation ends?

7. Rank the qualities in this chapter in order of their importance to you when considering someone to marry:

_____ humble

_____ forgiving

_____ handles conflict in a healthy way

_____ communicates well

_____ prays

_____ skilled in the art of friendship

12

Is Anybody in Charge?

A few generations ago, there was little, if any, disagreement on gender roles in marriage, but we live in a different age today. The problem is, while gender roles within church and marriage are discussed thoroughly in seminaries and select social media outlets, few dating couples are aware of this issue and fewer still discuss it. In fact, younger generations (I realize that some of you reading this may be as old as I am) have been brought up to treat gender distinction with the same disgust as racial discrimination.

Seeking first the kingdom of God means our first goal is to build a marriage that honors God *as He designed it*, assuming that He knows best. But Christians now disagree on how to translate some of the Scriptures that traditionally have been taken to describe the perhaps different roles of husband and wife. While I have my own opinions on this matter, what's even more important is whether you agree with each other on how to apply these Scriptures. If you disagree on this issue, I think it's a deal breaker.

One of the top complaints I hear from thirty- and fortysomething wives is that their husbands aren't acting as "spiritual leaders," but some now question the appropriateness of the very concept. Gender roles are based on two differing views of marriage that theologians call "egalitarian" or "complementarian."

In general, the egalitarian viewpoint sees no such thing as gender roles in marriage. In this view, God doesn't call men to servant leadership; that's religious cultural conditioning more than it is scriptural. Every couple should make their own decisions about who does what best, divide up the responsibilities, and base their marriage on individual strengths and weaknesses. The husband isn't expected to be a leader but rather a fifty-fifty partner. The thought of him leading is, in itself, somewhat offensive and demeaning to his wife. Nobody has the final say, and neither partner has more responsibility than the other to provide, guide, and protect.

Every verse that seems to suggest men have a leadership role at home and in marriage (1 Cor. 11:3; Eph. 5:22–24; Col. 3:18–19; 1 Tim. 5:11–15; Titus 2:4–5; 1 Pet. 3:1–7) can be explained away by context, later additions to the original manuscripts, a more refined study of the original language, or a "trajectory" view of Scripture that suggests the New Testament realized the first century wasn't ready for egalitarianism, so it simply laid the foundation for it in future generations. The fact that the church used to think that men needed to step up as leaders at home and in the church is a historical weakness that needs to be discarded and explained away, not a biblical truth to be applied today.

In the complementarian viewpoint, God has given the husband a role of loving servant leadership. Complementary does not mean a man is more capable or valuable than a woman; rather, it seeks to describe the complementary roles men and women play to best reveal to the world the relationship between Christ and the church. Complementarians believe that the same verses cited in the previous paragraph are too numerous, written to too many churches, and even written by too many different authors to explain each one away. Reasonable complementarians believe that the Bible describes the role of the husband more as one of *responsibility* than *privilege*, without condoning the patriarchal or societal oppression of women. It also has no resemblance to the 1950s stereotype of a subservient wife who appears inferior to her husband on many levels.

With a truly biblical view of complementarianism, the wife might work outside the home, especially since Proverbs 31 refers to a wife who earns income. Colossians 3:19 also makes it clear that a "biblical" husband will listen to his wife and take her welfare into consideration. In fact, the way Paul describes marriage in Ephesians 5 means that complementarianism should lead men to do what's best for their wives over what they prefer for themselves. It does call men to reject passivity and to step up in their homes and marriages so that they love their wives in the same way that Christ loved the church and gave Himself up for it. This is what many believe the Bible teaches in the passages cited above, taken together and applied throughout the majority of the church's history until the previous generation or so.

Because of the fierce debate between these two positions and the way each gets stereotyped negatively, "complementarian" and "egalitarian" labels aren't all that helpful anymore. This is a matter of scriptural interpretation, and many Christians are finding themselves smack in the middle rather than wanting to identify with either camp. However, I do encourage you to spend a date night going over the Scriptures listed above, making sure there's general agreement between the two of you over what kind of marriage honors these inspired words of instruction. I think it's vital that you and a future spouse come to the same understanding. Here's why.

The Importance of Alignment

The problems with disagreement on this issue may not be what you think. Wives in complementarian marriages may manage finances, and husbands in such marriages may do much or even all of the cooking, just as many egalitarian husbands can be strong leaders. This debate often gets muddled by superficial, nonbiblical issues that aren't concrete or even helpful. It's often sidetracked with silly stereotypes—as if all complementarian men are abusive chauvinist pigs and all egalitarian men are spineless effeminate liberals.

Most of the common misconceptions about gender roles aren't at a biblical level. Who handles finances, who cleans and cooks, who chooses where to go on vacation, or even what will constitute 99.9 percent of the general household decisions—biblical gender roles don't usually speak to such issues. But the notion of gender roles does affect marital expectations such as how to raise children, what church you will attend, and how one views Scripture, all of which matters *deeply*.

Repeated conflicts arise from a woman who expects her husband to be a spiritual leader and yet marries a man who finds such a concept demeaning to women. If her husband doesn't believe in spiritual leadership, she can't expect him to become a spiritual leader. If finances get tight, she might expect him to step up and get a better-paying job. He might think, "Why don't *I* stay home, and *you* get a second job?" If she wants a spiritual leader, she needs to marry a guy who has that mind-set.

Guys who feel called to lead in their homes but aren't allowed to do so will feel emasculated. Women who want their guys to lead but marry guys who don't will feel frustrated. Women who strongly adhere to the egalitarian perspective but who marry complementarians may not feel respected and will have serious problems when it comes to how the children are raised.

In a mixed egalitarian/complementarian marriage, both the husband and wife will likely try to treat the other according to their perceived sense of marital duties, but those duties won't be received as such—they'll be resented. What a complementarian woman finds loving and respectful, an egalitarian woman might find demeaning and frustrating, and vice versa. Since this rises to the level of biblical application, it must be frustrating to the extreme to aspire toward something your spouse finds offensive.

People who disagree on this issue can still worship the same God, but it will be difficult for them to raise the same kids or operate the same household.

Your Chance for a Do-Over

Because I believe that God designed marriage in part to make us holy even more than to make us happy, I also believe that He designed marriage in part to confront the pride of both men and women. In the complementarian worldview, men have their pride challenged in marriage by being commanded to put their wives' needs and comfort above their own (Eph. 5:25–29). Suddenly, another person not only has a legitimate claim but a *prior* claim on a man's time, money, and affections.

The Bible challenges the pride of women by telling them to learn how to love their husbands and be helpers to them (Titus 2:4, among others). The Bible doesn't tell women in general to submit to men in general, but some passages seem to suggest that wives submit to husbands (though some will debate what "submit" means).

The complementarian model, in my view, builds on this soul-shaping reality of learning to die to ourselves. It will help each partner grow in humility, service, understanding, and selflessness. It's a spiritually rich climate for potential character growth in Christlikeness.

Having said this, complementarianism taken too far can become extreme and even abusive, certainly demeaning to women. Philosophically, you don't want to necessarily reject something just because it has been abused, however. A husband who claims "privilege" is a husband who doesn't understand the meaning of the word *martyr*.

My daughter went through a college class that discussed gender roles, and her response was intriguing. "Dad," she said, "if most men treated their wives like I see you treating Mom, and most brothers treated their sisters like Graham treats us, more women would be complementarians. Most women want to be treated like that. But that's not the case. A lot of people my age have seen a lot of unhealthy marriages, and they don't want that. I think most women want what you and Graham offer, but they're rejecting what they've seen in their own homes."

I say this not to exalt my son or myself; there are a million things I could have done better as a husband and father. But seriously consider this: when you get married, you get a chance to create an entirely new family. Don't let unhealthy family-of-origin issues unduly shape the construction of your new immediate family, *especially as a reaction*.

In essence, God is giving you an opportunity for a do-over *based on His Word*, not your experience. (I know there are some rich, deeply intimate, God-honoring egalitarian marriages as well.) Have your mind washed by Scripture, allow your heart to be cleansed by God's forgiveness and acceptance, and aspire to make the healthiest, most God-honoring choice possible. You didn't choose to be born into your family; you *do* get to choose the person you marry to create your next family.

God is giving you an opportunity

for a do-over *based on His*

Word, not your experience.

Gender roles also influence how you raise your daughters and what values you choose to instill in your sons. This issue goes down to the very core of a person's identity. In my view, it also directly affects the way you read, study, and view the Bible, but that raises other contentious issues I don't want to get into right now.

Agree about this before you get married. Read and study the biblical passages we've mentioned. Reflect on and pray over them. Come to the best conclusion you can arrive at, and be wary if both of you don't agree.

One more crucial point: ultimately, this is a biblical issue more than it is a matter of what you want. It's not appropriate to ask, "What role sounds better to *me*?" Rather, you should ask, "What scriptural perspective seems clearest?" After you reach that conclusion, find a believer who agrees with you. Some issues can be compromised on; this one is a bit dangerous to ignore.

Searching Questions

1. Which type of marriage (egalitarian or complementarian) did your family of origin most closely
   resemble? Which one most closely resembles what
   you believe marriage should be?
2. Do you need to do more study to determine what
   the Bible teaches in this area? How can you go
   about that?
3. Discuss the most likely problems that will erupt if
   a complementarian marries an egalitarian, or vice
   versa.
4. How might these views affect the way you would
   raise and train your children?

13

You're Looking for a Complement, Not a Clone

Through the years at marriage conferences, church presentations, and the like, I've heard at least a dozen married couples tell a large group how it's impossible for two people to be more opposite from each other. In heaven, I hope God will put all of them in the same room and let them battle it out for supremacy.

They always come to the same point: they still have a strong marriage even though they're not technically "compatible." The danger in you thinking this way as a single is that there are different *forms* of compatibility, and some forms matter more than others. It's worth considering this issue, since lack of compatibility is one of the most frequently cited causes of divorce.

It's typical for opposites to attract, so don't worry about that. Compatibility that matters isn't about sameness as much as it's about having the most important things in common, beginning with a shared vision for life. Sincere appreciation and genuine respect for your future spouse matter far more than similarity.

Here's the challenge you need to overcome as a single who wants to know if you and your intended are compatible: the process of dating and looking for a mate, combined with the early days of marriage, provide an *artificial* sense of compatibility. In the early days of your relationship, compatibility is artificially enhanced via sexual chemistry. Infatuation and immediate attraction are so strong, compatibility or incompatibility barely even register. You both feel crazy about each other—how could you *not* be compatible? And then when you move toward marriage and start planning a wedding, the ceremony itself gives you something in common. You plan it, talk about it, and divide up tasks to make it happen. After the wedding you start setting up a house, move into a new apartment or neighborhood, and try to join two lives. That also joins you in a common task and gives you something to talk about. If this is a first marriage, you're likely to start raising kids. That's a big thing to have in common and requires a lot of communication. But eventually the kids are going to leave the two of you alone together. That's when the abundance or lack of compatibility will either take you to new heights or appear like a giant sinkhole that sucks the life out of your relationship.

The empty-nest years slay a lot of marriages because the couple has slowly grown apart. They may have never shared that much in common other than having once "fallen in love" and gone through common life tasks while sharing the same address.

The good news is that when Matthew 6:33 is a shared value, you are spiritually compatible, and that's enough to hold a marriage together. However, other forms of compatibility will certainly make the relationship more *pleasant*.

Relational Compatibility

The foundation of relational compatibility is a shared appreciation for each other's *personality* and *character*. My wife isn't like me, but I *like* who she is. There are many areas in which I'm glad she's not like me. What would be a problem is if those areas annoyed me or caused me to disrespect her.

I'm the introvert and Lisa is the extrovert, which means I'd usually like to leave social events about an hour before Lisa does. When we're traveling on speaking trips, I don't mind at all crashing on the bed in the hotel room to watch some sports, read, and relax. Lisa can't stand staying in a hotel room if she's not sleeping. She researches museums, parks, restaurants, *anything* to get us out of the hotel room. I rarely *feel* like going out with her after speaking, but when I do, I am almost always glad I did. Lisa's differences help keep me from collapsing into the worst parts of myself.

When it comes to evaluating relational compatibility, authors Ben Young and Samuel Adams remind us that personality doesn't change; we grow and evolve, but we don't become completely new people. *The person you marry is the person you're going to be married to.* That sounds elementary, but a lot of people don't believe that. They fall for someone's *potential*, thinking the person they're marrying is going to change into someone who is substantially different. They thus marry someone with whom they might be somewhat "incompatible," hoping that they'll *become* compatible.

Do you want to be married for the rest of your life to someone who irritates or embarrasses you? Don't laugh—people do this all the time. They marry someone like that because they think it's time to get married, or they think it's the best they can do, or they get infatuated and rush into an ill-suited marriage—and soon resent who their spouse is. Then they try to change the person. Good luck with that.

Finding someone you enjoy being with is far more important (and less narcissistic) than finding someone who is just like you. According to Young and Adams, "It is not necessary or even healthy to find someone with the same personality traits. The issue has to do with your ability to accept and adapt to your partner's personality style, assuming it will not change."[1] In other words, you're looking for a complement, not a clone.

You can be an introvert who is happily married to an extrovert, as long as you like the fact that your spouse will be the life of the party. It will be a good thing if you want to be challenged to get out a bit more. But if you truly want to spend most nights at home, consider marrying another introvert. Young and Adams explain that bringing out the best in each other requires mutual *respect* and *appreciation*. If you don't respect and appreciate your partner, you're not compatible. You'll never become a true, heartfelt companion of someone who bugs you, consistently embarrasses you, or for whom you have little respect. I know you love your boyfriend or girlfriend. But do you also *like* him? Is he the kind of person you enjoy being around? If it wasn't for the sexual chemistry, and if you didn't feel romantically inclined toward her, would you still enjoy her company?

We grow and evolve, but we don't become completely new people. *The person you marry is the person you're going to be married to.*

Companionship is the relational heart that pumps blood into your marriage. People are often drawn to each other through sexual chemistry, and while there is a certain excitement in this aspect of relating, you'll be companions 99 percent more than you'll perform as sexual partners. Furthermore, sexual chemistry rises and falls far more wildly than does relational companionship, which usually grows deeper over time. Two companions can have at least a satisfactory sexual relationship if they are motivated by kindness and love. But a satisfactory sexual relationship does *not* guarantee relational compatibility.

Remember, you're seeking someone you are *eager to live with*, not *put up with*. If you feel like you are already tolerating your partner's personality for the sake of the relationship mainly because your feelings for him or her are so strong, proceed with caution.

Recreational Compatibility

There is a level of sameness that can be helpful, however, and that's in the area of how you like to play and relax. Most people can't afford to go on numerous expensive vacations. Maybe it'll be different for you, but here's where compatibility can become a serious issue. Lisa and I are friends with a couple who go to Saint Martin every year. They lie in the sun for hours, get a massage in the afternoon (*every* afternoon), have an early dinner, and call it a day. They might do one or two activities in the course of the fourteen days they spend there, but no more than that, and only if they want to.

Visiting the same place and doing the same thing every year would drive my wife bonkers. She lands on an island and thinks, *How can I explore every last blessed inch of this place in the mere 336 hours I have left?*

It's not just vacation; it's how you spend your evenings, weekends, and holidays. When both people really enjoy antique shopping or gardening or scouring bookstores or following their favorite football team or being at church as much as possible or running marathons together, that kind of common activity *increases* intimacy as time passes. Shared interests fertilize commitment, satisfaction, and communication.

Unfortunately, modern life usually separates couples. Since few married partners work together, most of us are required to be apart from each other during the most active hours of the day, at least five days a week. If you also have to separate in order to fully enjoy your rest and recreation, when are you going to connect? And can you truly connect when you don't really like what your spouse is most interested in?

Older remarried couples tend to do a bit better in seeking out compatibility in this area, in large part because they have more experience. A lot of twentysomethings don't really know what they like to do on vacation in the midst of working a full-time job. This is a tough one to imagine, so I'm downplaying it a bit for the younger crowd, but it's certainly something to consider.

Environmental Compatibility

To stimulate your thinking and discussion, consider three real-life scenarios of couples who found themselves in heart-wrenching situations where one or both partners had to make serious compromises they'd never considered before they got married.

A fifty-something man was a leading prospect from his party to run for president of the United States. His wife didn't want to move to Washington, DC, nor did she want to endure such a nationally public stage. Though advisors urged him to run, though people circulated petitions asking him to run, though numerous pundits said he very well could win if he ran, in the end he didn't become a candidate. His closest friends and advisors gave one reason for his decision: his wife's opposition.

Nia steadily rose through the ranks of a company until she got an offer she never even imagined: a prime executive-in-training position at the national office. Her employers were clearly grooming her for a VP spot sometime in the future. There was one major problem: her husband planned on taking over the family business in the south, and Nia's company expected her to move to Chicago. She and her husband had never talked about this possibility before they got married: when the reality of achieving their dreams collided, who got to pursue his or her dream first?

A young couple asked me to referee their disagreement. He wanted to go overseas to do missions work. She didn't. They had only been married for nine months, so I naturally asked, "Didn't you talk about this before you got married?"

He responded, "We thought we had ..."

I can tell you this: if you marry someone who doesn't want to go overseas, *that spouse will win that argument every time.* You *can't* force (or even cajole) someone to go overseas and expect the marriage and ministry to prosper. If God has called you overseas, it is your spiritual duty to marry someone who has some experience overseas so your intended knows what he or she is signing up for. Otherwise, you are putting your life call in jeopardy.

All three of these scenarios contain a common truth: your spouse will have enormous veto power over where you live and what you do. Right now, all you can think about is just being together, but the time will come when simply being together isn't enough. You will also care passionately about what you're doing when you're *not* together—your forty- to sixty-hour workweek.

Have you talked about where you might live, what you might want to do, not just in the next few years but also a couple of decades from now? Have you been honest about what you'll *never* agree to do or where you'll *never* agree to live?

Choosing where you'll live goes far beyond international/national discussions, of course. There is a vast difference between a life lived in Manhattan, New York, and one lived in Coeur d'Alene, Idaho. There is nothing morally superior about wanting to live on a farm, in a city apartment, or in a house in the suburbs. But if you don't agree, that's a pretty major challenge to overcome.

If you were born in the Midwest and can't imagine another life, respect that. Some Midwest girls fall for a city boy and, in the abstract, living in the city can sound romantic and exotic. But when they actually try to live in a one-room apartment that costs more than their parents' mortgage, breathe dirty air for six months, hear sirens blaring all day (and all night), pass panhandlers every time they go to the grocery store (which they have to walk to or take public transportation to get to and carry the groceries home in their arms), they start to go crazy. Similarly, a guy who revels in city life—restaurants being open at all hours, the energy that never dissipates, the ever-full menu of entertainment options—would pull his hair out trying to live in a suburb that essentially rolls up the streets at 7:00 p.m.

If you've never lived in the city and your potential spouse is set on it, do yourself a favor. Rent an apartment for a few months and try it out. (Vacation rental sites make this really easy to do now!) You won't know until you do it if you can stand it. Similarly, if your spouse dreams of a suburban lifestyle, try moving to a small town or the Midwest on a trial basis. Having lived in the Pacific Northwest, the area around Washington, DC, and Houston, Texas, I can attest that those are three *very* different lives.

Family Compatibility

The roar sounded like a riot. While biking through the streets of Maastricht in the Netherlands, my wife and I thought we saw a street protest coming our way.

"What do you think we should do?" Lisa asked me.

"Ride toward it to find out what's going on, of course."

The crowd grew larger and louder; the air was filled with electricity. As we got closer, we laughed.

Hundreds of kids poured out of an elementary school that was ending its day. The children were greeted by a wall of mothers waiting to walk them home.

There's something about being on the other side of the globe, in a town you've never been in before, and seeing something so intimate going on—kids running into their mothers' arms, speaking a language you can't understand but don't need to, that makes you celebrate life as God designed it. The kids were showing off artwork, explaining how they got a hole in their pants, talking about an upcoming test. It wasn't difficult to figure out what they were saying, even though we didn't understand a word of it.

This is more than a discussion about political correctness; you need to be in agreement about many important issues related to who and how you will raise your future children. Men, if you want your kids to have a mother who greets them at the end of the school day and walks them home, make sure you marry a woman who wants that too. Women, if you want to be that mom, make sure you marry a man who shows the economic capability of affording you that freedom. If you want your husband to be the one at home to greet the kids, you'd better talk about that as well. Are you both okay with that little kid running into the arms of a nanny or grandma?

Who is going to raise your kids? Are both of you committed to being home by a certain time and keeping the weekends free? (If so, that will keep both of you from accepting certain jobs.) Is one of you okay with being home alone with the kids on occasion?

Will you spend Christmas and Thanksgiving with your own kids or extended families? Okay, *which* extended family? Would you prefer to attend a large church or a small church? Why? What if your spouse insists on "house church" or "no church"?

Do you value family meals or watching the news on television while you eat? Have you talked about your kids' education: homeschooling, private schooling, public schooling, sacrificing for college? Lisa and I gladly scrimped on retirement savings to put our kids through three private colleges; most of our friends (and every financial advisor we talked to) thought our doing so was foolish. It's no big deal to disagree with your friends on this; it's a huge problem to disagree with your spouse.

Ideological Compatibility

This one is a bit tricky because it depends on how dearly you hold your opinions. I've heard of married couples where one spouse is an ardent conservative or liberal and the other spouse doesn't really care about politics. That's not much of a problem. But if both care about politics enthusiastically and find themselves on opposite sides, sparks can fly.

The same is true theologically. Some spouses don't have a preference between Methodist, Baptist, Presbyterian, or Roman Catholic and couldn't even tell you what doctrine sets each one apart. But when one spouse is a "cessationist" (believing the miraculous gifts ended with the apostles) and one is Pentecostal, you're going to have a difficult time finding a church you both like.

How important is it to you that your spouse agree with you politically and theologically? If it matters, talk about these issues beforehand.

Put It on Pause

I know—this is a *lot* to discuss and think about, but that's partly what dating is for. Now I'm going to ask you to do something that may feel even more painful: when you get close to becoming engaged, put any public announcement on delay for a few weeks and spend several sessions talking through all these issues *again* with someone else present. The reason I say this is that couples who are in love have an amazing ability to hear what they want to hear. Remember the would-be missionary who *thought* he and his wife had talked about living overseas?

Bring up anything you can think of. An occasional disagreement won't doom the relationship, so don't be too scared. But consistent incompatibility—in major areas—that can't be resolved is something you'd be foolish to ignore. You need to find a third party who loves you enough to point out these incompatibilities as they arise.

I once worked with a couple where the husband-to-be imagined a career in the military. The wife-to-be, when asked to be honest, admitted that she never saw herself as a military wife and didn't want to be one. I put them together with a military chaplain who could help them understand the ramifications of their decision. They were within months of the wedding *and hadn't dealt with this*. It's not uncommon at all for me to come across couples who shut their eyes to potential major conflicts. If you compromise on too many of these issues, or even on one really big issue, you risk fighting resentment for the rest of your life.

Remember: you don't have to make this one relationship work if it's not a good fit. Yes, every couple has to make certain compromises, but it's not wrong to want a certain level of happiness; in fact, it's wise to pursue general compatibility. While incompatibility is grounds for ending an engagement or dating relationship, it's *not* biblical grounds to pursue a divorce. So why not seriously examine your compatibility *before* you take the vows instead of after? If you make a foolish choice of a marriage partner, the Bible is going to ask you to live with the consequences.

Searching Questions

1. How common do you think it is that some people marry their partners for their potential—who they might become—rather than for who they really are? Do you think people will change substantially (in fundamental ways) after they get married?
2. Why do you think it's important to marry someone you don't just love but you also like and respect? What are the dangers of marrying someone who embarrasses you?
3. How important is recreation time to you—evenings, weekends, vacations, and holidays? How important are various activities to you on those days? Are there any that you wouldn't (or shouldn't) be willing to compromise on?
4. Do you think two people could enjoy a marriage in which they have little in common recreationally?
5. Thinking about twenty years from now, is there anywhere you think you absolutely would not want to live (city, suburbs, rural, foreign country, etc.)?
6. Do you envision one parent staying home with your kids, using day care, hiring a nanny, or trying to equally balance careers and child-rearing? What arrangement(s) would not be acceptable to you?
7. If Christians recognize they're starting to make many compromises in order to consider someone they're romantically inclined toward, how can they work through their concerns in a responsible way?

14

Dating with Intention

Dating can be a dangerous dance. Most of us want to be truly known and accepted, but we're afraid. If you see the real me, will you run away? Am I even worth being known? Will the real me bore you? Scare you? Repulse you? And so we hide. Some of us want to be married more than we want to be known so we start trying to please the other person more than we try to get to know him or her. We aim to get our girlfriend or boyfriend to like us, rather than intentionally help this person truly understand us. In such a "dance," we never become truly known and thus live with the anxiety that if we do become known, our partner might leave.

Your job is to break through this facade and truly get to know the person you're planning to marry, as well as help your intended get to know the real you. Unless you're thoughtful about how you date and what you do on your dates, dating may not reveal the real you or the real him or her. Going to the movies, biking through the park, eating out—of course that kind of activity is going to create a certain level of affection. But it's not real life; it's often not even real relating. It's just playing. It doesn't tell you much about how a man could face a medical or vocational crisis, what kind of courage a woman has, what values each person lives by, or what spiritual pursuit drives the other person. Some dates need to be purposeful, designed to ferret out your boyfriend's or girlfriend's character.

Your mission is to truly get to know this other person, and that takes intentional effort. Here's what to do to get there.

Trinity Talk

You know why so many relationships slowly wither into nothingness? They stop seeking first the kingdom of God. There's no overarching mission in the couple's lives beyond self-enjoyment. This entraps them in a life of petty battles and superficial cares. If a woman spends far more time picking out living room furniture than she does getting to know anyone who is spiritually lost or she becomes virtually consumed with getting a better office with a better view, that's not going to captivate any man for very long. When a man is more obsessed with becoming a scratch golfer than with being available to God, how could a woman not lose interest sooner rather than later? People grow bored with each other. If we have no grand passion and simply live for ourselves, we become boring.

What's the antidote? Seeking first the kingdom of God—not as a means but as an end in itself. Such a pursuit cultivates a fundamentally different form of sharing, the kind that comes first from relating to God. I call this "Trinity talk." When we pray and read Scripture, God reveals Himself to us. We see our motivations in a new light; we see sins, but God reveals them to us in the light of grace. We can humbly admit our weaknesses and gain a vision for a better future. We are energized to attempt great things for God. We *never* run out of things to talk about because we are becoming new people with new visions and new purpose. Instead of sharing small, stagnant lives that produce little personal growth and even less vision, we become dynamic people who are growing ever more like Christ and are regularly reignited in our passion to see God's work spread in the world.

My good friend Kevin Harney had been married for a number of years when God spoke to him about becoming "recklessly generous" toward a church-based need. He swallowed hard as he considered the actual amount he believed God was calling him to give. That much money would mean emptying out virtually all his and his wife's life savings.

When he came home from work, his wife, Sherry, explained how, during her morning jog, God had prepared her to "give generously" to the same project. She gulped and mentioned a number, fearing Kevin's reaction. It was the exact amount that her husband felt God had placed on his heart.

While this episode depleted their bank account, it filled their marital intimacy to overflowing. They were growing in God *together*, facing the excitement of life on the edge of serving God *together*. The last thing you would say about Kevin and Sherry *over thirty years* into their marriage with each other is that they are bored with each other.

It's not just about what we do for God; it's about who we become in God. When I keep relating to God, I literally become a different person, so there's always someone new for my wife to get to know. The same is true for me with her. Just recently, my wife prayed a brilliant prayer for some hurting parents. The Spirit of God within her was so mightily evident it renewed my love for her all over again, and I thanked God for the privilege of being married to a woman who is growing in the grace of prayer.

Seeking first the kingdom of God means that your communication needs to become three-way: bring God into the center of it. What is God revealing, what is God doing, and what is God forgiving, counseling, encouraging you with?

On your dates, find out what God is doing in and through your friend. Does he even hear from God? Is she aware of her sin? Does he have any sense of mission? Can the two of you inspire and encourage each other to become more focused on seeking God's kingdom together?

Watch with Me

When you're with your boyfriend or girlfriend, *pay attention*. How does she treat her family? What's his relationship like with his parents? His siblings? How does she act around kids? How does he treat "invisible" people—waiters, janitors, and the like? If a guy is too lazy to bus his own table at McDonald's or return a grocery store cart to its rightful place in the parking lot, what makes you think he won't leave his stuff around the house, expecting someone else to pick it up?

Here's the painful reality when you enter any dating relationship: your partner can't be completely 100 percent altruistic. She wants something from you. Maybe he wants to marry you. Maybe she wants to make out with you. Maybe he just wants to make you like him. You can assume that she's on her best behavior with you. So whatever your boyfriend or girlfriend does *for you*—buying flowers, baking food, offering encouragement—comes from somewhat mixed motives.

The only way to know true character, then, is to watch your friend with someone else. Women, if you're with a guy who wants to be in ministry but he's criticizing every pastor and sermon he hears, I guarantee you that five years after he's married to you he'll have a whole lot of criticism about your role as a wife. Guys, if you're around a woman who does kind things for you *but no one else*, the days of her doing kind things for you are severely numbered—probably within weeks of the wedding, if you want to know the truth.

I reconnected with a college friend I hadn't talked to in years. When I asked about his marriage, he laughed about how his wife and told me "you may recall" (I did) how much time she spent in the library studying as a student; he related that now she spends just as much time preparing for her lessons as a school teacher. He does the lion's share of taking care of their daughter because his wife has so much to prepare for each day's workload. He doesn't mind, but the point is worth making: who she was as a student revealed who she would be vocationally as a teacher.

Date with your eyes open. Get into ministry situations, family situations, maybe even stressful situations, to see how he or she reacts. If one little thing goes wrong and ruins the whole date, you can bet that on a future family vacation there is going to be a whole lot of drama and not much rest, because something always goes wrong on a family vacation.

Most modern dating focuses on how two people treat *each other*. That's not particularly helpful, especially in the flush of infatuation. You've got to get outside the relationship to get inside the motivations and heart of the person you're thinking about marrying.

Go down Memory Lane

Keeping with this theme—how to test a serious dating relationship—explore what your boyfriend or girlfriend was like *before* meeting you. Did he enjoy sports? Did she attend church? Did he do the things the two of you enjoy doing together now? Without letting on what you're doing, purposefully try to crack the code of your beloved's past, as that past is a fairly good indicator of the future.

If your future spouse didn't go to church before he or she met you, it's unlikely church will be a priority after the wedding. If that person pretended to like sports or museums or cooking, it won't take long until the playacting ends. *Get to know your potential spouse's past so that you can get a read on your future.* Be very suspicious of any major change.

Talk to his or her siblings, parents, friends. Ask to see old photo albums, or do a social media search through your intended's past posts. You've got to be a bit discreet here; don't sound like an FBI agent interrogating a witness. But informally ask questions in casual conversations to get a little deeper into your potential spouse's psyche. The fewer surprises you have after you marry someone, the better.

As you consider these and other issues, I'd recommend Dr. Paul Friesen's book *Before You Save the Date: 21 Questions to Help You Marry with Confidence.* Going through Paul's book will assist you in getting inside your partner's heart.

Get to know your potential spouse's past

so that you can get a read on your future.

Pray

I know some people counsel that unmarried couples *shouldn't* pray together, as it might create an intimacy that leads to sexual activity. If you've found this to be the case, perhaps you should only pray when others are present. For my own part, I'd want to be alone with someone before the Lord and hear the concerns of her heart to get a better read on who she really is in Christ.

How does your girlfriend or boyfriend talk to God? Is He a friend or some distant stranger that the person you love almost seems afraid of or embarrassed by? Do you pick up a heartfelt passion, a sense of someone who is familiar with this conversation, or do you feel like you're listening in on someone who is talking to you and trying to impress you more than actually talking to God? What does she pray for and about? Does he have a concern for others, do her prayers reveal a trivial life and petty concerns, or is he swept up by God's compassion for others?

Of course, people can still "act" when they pray, but if you pray with them more than a couple of times, you'll begin to get a better feel for where they're at with the Lord.

Infatuated couples invariably try to change for each other. Remember, during infatuation you become obsessed with getting and keeping your heart's desire. Because you so desperately want the relationship to work, you will find yourself astonishingly open to making little compromises and *temporary* changes in your lifestyle and even personality to accommodate the relationship. This motivation almost always fades with the infatuation. To counter this, it's essential that you date *with intention*; get behind the mask to find out who this person really is, and please, let your boyfriend or girlfriend see you as well.

Searching Questions

1. Since most of us want to be known and to truly know someone else, why do we so often hide from each other and even mislead each other in romantic relationships?

2. How might a "current grand passion" keep feeding a marriage? What are the dangers of marrying someone without such a shared passion?

3. How important do you think it is for someone to be not just a Christian but *growing* as a Christian? How can you tell if someone you are dating is stagnant or maturing?

4. Do you think it's fair to suggest that the way a man treats his sisters and mom might reflect on his character as a husband, or the way a woman treats her brothers or father might hold clues to the kind of wife she would be? In what ways?

5. Are there dangers involved in dating partners praying together? What might some of the benefits be? How can this be done appropriately? (Or should it?)

15

Your Brain on Sex

Seth and Gabrielle got legally married early on a Sunday morning in Houston, Texas. They didn't have sex until Wednesday night, about eighty hours later.

Let me explain.

The young couple originally planned to get married in Mexico, but Mexican law requires a Mexican clergyman, Mexican blood tests, and a waiting period in-country for the wedding to be legalized. Seth and Gabrielle wanted to get married by their own pastor, not a strange clergyman, so they had a short legal ceremony in advance, signed the papers, and caught a flight for Mexico.

Gabrielle told Seth, "This doesn't mean a thing until my daddy walks me down the aisle," by which she meant the "official" ceremony in Mexico.

Seth wasn't quite as eager to waive such informalities. He had signed a legal document. A pastor he respected had declared him married. He was paying for a great honeymoon suite at a resort in Mexico, so why, on Sunday, Monday, and Tuesday nights, was Gabrielle sleeping alone in that beautiful, spacious room designed especially for romance—and he was down the hall, sharing a bed in a small room with his dad? To make matters even more painful,

Seth's father decided to use these final hours to dispense "honeymoon advice" in anticipation of the big day.

I'm not asking you to debate whether Gabrielle should have given Seth a room key. Though it was more than a little frustrating for Seth, he admits in hindsight that it was "special" waiting until after the formal ceremony. But you might be thinking, *Isn't all this a little outdated? Come on, this is the twenty-first century! Nobody waits until they get married anymore.*

I share this story because I want you to look at sex and dating in a way that perhaps you never have before. You have heard the sermons and read the biblical verses about not mistreating each other: "It is God's will that you should be sanctified: that you should avoid sexual immorality; that each of you should learn to control your own body in a way that is holy and honorable, not in passionate lust like the pagans, who do not know God; *and that in this matter no one should wrong or take advantage of a brother or sister*" (1 Thess. 4:3–6).

Sexual desire makes us extremely vulnerable; Paul urges the church not to take advantage of that vulnerability. That biblical directive is reason enough not to get involved sexually before you marry. But understanding God's purposes for sexuality should reinforce your commitment. God knows what He's talking about. His plan is brilliant. The more I think about and study God's purpose for sexuality, the more amazed I become about this incredible invention He designed—and the wisdom He dispenses in telling us how to use it.

I'm a huge fan of sex because when it is used appropriately, it does amazing and marvelous things for a married couple. But when it is experienced outside of God's designed context, it can lead you to make a poor *lifelong* choice all because of a *few moments* of pleasure.

This chapter is about setting yourself up to use sex to serve your future marriage (safeguarding your own happiness and pleasure) and avoiding letting sex sabotage your search for a wise marriage partner.

Brains and Bonding

If you scope out a female brain, you'll find that a woman may have up to ten times more oxytocin at any given time than your average man. Oxytocin is a neurochemical* that creates or at least reflects feelings of warmth, affection, bonding, and intimacy. And the fact that women have more of it explains a lot about their general comfort with relating to others emotionally.

There is one time, however, when a male's level of oxytocin approaches that of a female. Immediately following a sexual encounter, the man experiences a surge of oxytocin that may even catch him off guard, which explains why single gals are sometimes shocked when a man they barely know blurts out "I think I love you" following a hasty sexual encounter. It's the chemicals talking!

Within marriage, this flood of oxytocin is a brilliant attachment device. God knows infatuation will fade. After we're married, we need something that will renew our affection for each other on a regular basis. One of the most hurtful things young wives tell me is that they resent how before the wedding they seemed to be their husband's number-one priority but after the wedding they dropped to number three or four. There's just something about the male psyche that after we "get the girl" we move on to the next challenge. Suddenly, the new husband is focused on his career, his golf handicap, his hunting, his fantasy football league, you name it.

---

* Technically, it's a "neuropeptide."

God is not unaware of this. He knows we men are not altruistic by nature and may grow to ignore our wives. Since our wives are also God's daughters—and God is passionately devoted to His daughters' welfare—He brilliantly created the hormone behind the sex drive that healthy men carry plenty of. And God designed marriage with the instruction that the only legitimate place sexual satisfaction can be found is with one's wife. So the husband has a literal physical reminder—"I need my wife"—and when that need is expressed and met according to God's explicit instructions, the man's brain is flooded with a bonding neurochemical that reignites his affection and passion for his wife, while the wife gets a thrilling orgasm that has been shown to improve her immune system, help her get a better night's sleep, lower her blood pressure, and also feel closer to her husband.

Again, within marriage, this is brilliant. A wise man soon learns that to be sexually intimate with his wife requires maintaining emotional and spiritual intimacy as well, so he has a physical drive that can keep him from getting complacent relationally (unless, of course, he turns to a cheap substitute such as pornography).

However, before marriage, what proves immensely helpful to *cement* a relationship proves equally unhelpful to *test* a relationship. If your infatuation is fading but you become sexually intimate, you're renewing your neurochemical affection for each other. You're assigning that feeling of intimacy to each other when you should still be testing and evaluating the relationship, not cementing it. Even apart from the moral aspect, premarital sex is a foolish thing to do for this reason: just when you need to be most alert to make the best choice you can possibly make, sex creates a neurochemical fog that will confuse you. You're going to feel like you want to stay with that person, even if you mentally understand that it's not a particularly wise match. *You're literally launching a neurochemical war against your mental reasoning.* Dr. Paul Friesen boldly stated, "There is no area that blinds couples more to their challenges than premature sexual involvement."[1]

I'm a huge fan of sex because when it is used appropriately, it does amazing and marvelous things for a married couple. But when it is experienced outside of God's designed context, it can lead you to make a poor *lifelong* choice all because of a *few moments* of pleasure.

Any way you look at it, sexual involvement before marriage is unhelpful. It will confuse you as you evaluate the relationship. If the relationship proves unworthy of a lifetime commitment, having been sexual will make the breakup more painful. You must train yourself to ignore what God created you to pay attention to. Learning to *disregard* this cement (which you must eventually do to break things off) will undercut the positive effects it has in marriage. It will dull your ability to sexually connect with the person you do marry. When you sexually reconnect, you feel the effects of the neurochemical cement.

The notion that this doesn't matter as much as trying out your "sexual compatibility" is misguided. Trust your Creator! God *designed* sex to be pleasurable and satisfying. He knew what He was doing and—no surprise—He succeeded. Sex can indeed be amazing. It's also a skill that can be learned, and that's what marriage allows, so if the two of you aren't "compatible" on your wedding night, you have a lifetime to get there.

Two people who genuinely care for each other and who are growing in the virtues of kindness and generosity will figure out how to please and keep on pleasing each other sexually. You don't have to "test" sex—believe me, it works! Enjoying sex with each other isn't a test of the relationship. That's like saying, "We know we were made for each other because we both think chocolate chip mint ice cream is delicious," or "we both think sunsets are beautiful." Join the club—so do millions of other people. In the same way, plenty of people could potentially bring you to the point of orgasm. And guess what? You'd enjoy those orgasms. God created you with skin that can be electrified with a light touch, nerve endings, genitals, and a brain that makes sex supremely pleasurable. In the end, all you've learned is that God is a good Creator and engineer. You haven't learned whether the person who manipulated your body to orgasm is capable of building a family with you.

Let me add another important point: even if, as a married couple, you eventually have sex three times a week (which is above average for couples married more than five years) the time you'll spend having sex will add up to less than one percent of your marriage. A fantastic one percent won't overcome a frustrating 99 percent; "sexually compatible" couples get divorced all the time.

And an occasionally frustrating one percent of your marriage won't doom your relationship if the other 99 percent of your marriage is satisfying and fulfilling.

Of course, staying sexually pure isn't easy. If your partner is a good potential match, it's going to be excruciatingly (and increasingly) difficult to stay sexually pure. If it's not difficult, in fact, you should take notice. Paul Friesen warns, "Some couples will boast that the physical purity part of their relationship is going well. 'We have no problem in this area,' they may say. If you have been dating for a while and are contemplating marriage and 'have no problem in this area,' you have a problem. You should be fighting with all your might to stay pure; you definitely should feel a strong sexual desire for each other."[2] The absence of sexual desire could be a serious indicator of underlying problems.

According to statistics, it's likely that you and your boyfriend or girlfriend have already been sexually intimate with each other. You might be thinking, *What now?*

Immediate sexual connection, like infatuation, fades. It puts you in a fog for a while, but couples who are sexually intimate break up all the time. I'm speaking here apart from the spiritual context, which we'll get to in just a moment. For the purposes of evaluating your relationship, decide from this point on that you're going to date God's way. You're going to stop what you've been doing and see if the relationship grows or suffers accordingly.

We also need to consider, which we'll do now, how to respond to a potential partner's sexual past.

Putting the Past behind You

We live in a sexually promiscuous age, so there are fewer and fewer single adults with a "perfect" sexual past. Nicholas Wolfinger, writing on behalf of the Institute for Family Studies, notes a huge divide from even the 1970s, when women getting married with one (very possibly their fiancé) or no prior sexual partners was 43%. Today, it's 22%. With the pressures of our highly-charged and over-sexualized media, then adding in things like pornography, erotica, and abuse, the reality is that most of us stumble into marriage with plenty of sexual brokenness. You will have to look long and far to find a person who doesn't have some sexual sin or hurt in his or her past. Just because you've sinned or been sinned against doesn't mean that God views you as damaged goods or that He doesn't want you to experience sexual fulfillment in marriage. He'll be the primary agent to help you heal so you can move on to a rewarding and intimacy-building sexual connection with your spouse.

But sex before marriage *does* create challenges we need to be honest about. God's forgiveness and grace don't mean that the *level* of a person's prior sexual involvement doesn't matter. It does. Wolfinger found that women with ten or more prior sexual partners were the most likely to get divorced; women with one to nine partners were less likely to get divorced; while women with zero to one were the least likely to get divorced.

Prior sexual sin can be forgiven, but the consequences can be severe. Sexual sin corrupts our minds and trains our brains and bodies in the wrong direction. When talking to couples, I have noticed a direct connection between a man and woman's level of sexual promiscuity and the sexual difficulties they have in their marriage. It doesn't have to be this way—we'll talk about why in a moment—but it often is, largely because people feel so ashamed of their past that they rarely deal with it. They just pretend the past didn't happen or act like it won't matter and then suffer the consequences accordingly, without ever drawing a line of connection between the lack of

YOUR BRAIN ON SEX   171

healing in their past and their sexual performance and enjoyment in
the present.

If sexual sin didn't have consequences, it seems unlikely that
God would forbid it. He is a gracious God, definitely not malicious,
and amazingly kind and generous. Directly rebelling against His
wisdom, doing nothing about it, and then expecting there to be no
consequences is worse than calling God a liar; it is calling Him a
pleasure-killing, malicious liar.

Because God is *not* a liar, we can face these very painful and
embarrassing issues and look boldly at our sin, admitting its ugliness
and its past power over us. In fact, we have confidence to face the
reality of our brokenness because we serve the all-powerful, victori-
ous King Jesus who died to cover the cost of our sin and who sent
His Holy Spirit to guide us into a new way of thinking, a new way
of feeling, and a new way of living. Jesus *died* to win this hope for
us. With this hope, we don't have to settle for anything less than
God's best. We can embrace it. God can and will help us overcome
the negative imprinting of our foolish choices. Let's look at how this
applies to "digital" sin (porn) and then past sexual experience.

The Porn Problem

Women, here's one of the challenges you face: because of the rise of
the internet, almost every guy has seen some porn, and many guys
have seen a lot. And guys, an increasing number of women have also
watched porn. The easy access and confusing messages of culture
tell you that porn is harmless and fun. But the producers of porn
have dramatically shaped the souls and expectations of millions of
single men and women. Sometimes women suffer even more shame
because they think they aren't "supposed" to be as into porn as guys
are. Shame keeps people silent, self-condemning, and trapped.

Nobody wins.

I have talked to many Christian fiancées who are devastated when they get into counseling and find out their future husband has a history with porn. You are right to be both concerned and cautious, but I hope you also understand this isn't a fair fight. When I was growing up, a person had to be a certain age to buy a pornographic magazine. Today, the internet offers salacious material freely, without making even a token attempt to protect young minds. I've worked with numerous God-fearing, honorable young men who got trapped in this struggle without even looking for it. Take any naturally curious twelve-year-old boy and tell him, "Press this button and you get to see what a naked woman looks like," and he can't push that button fast enough. It might not even be prurient—there's just a natural curiosity at play. Then tell him, "Now, press this button, and you'll get to see what sex looks like," and his curiosity will once again get the best of him. Some boys, exposed to something their souls aren't prepared to handle, will get a thrilling rush and then be ushered into a habit that will stick with them for perhaps the rest of their lives. Curiosity did more than kill the cat; it has captured a generation of boys.

And of course, it's not just young boys who are being targeted. A licensed counselor and friend of mine, Debra Fileta writes,

> Women struggle with porn, too, and it's on the rise. Various studies have even reported female porn use at 86%. As a licensed counselor, I regularly see the negative effects porn has on the female heart and brain. Porn wires you to sexually respond to a fictional perception of relationships, rather than the real thing. When paired with masturbation (which

it almost always is), it can commonly impair your ability to physically respond to sexual encounters with your future husband. It's the enemy of a healthy relationship. If you're a woman struggling with porn, I need you to know that you are not alone. Not even close. Sometimes the shame of porn use as a woman, buries you in it even deeper. But the key to healing is not shame, the key to healing is Christ. With a combination of professional counseling and boundaries surrounding your life, you can walk away in freedom from addiction, and begin the process of recalibrating your heart and mind. I've seen it happen time and time again. Don't wait another day because healing is yours for the taking.[3]

Dr. Patrick Carnes, a widely respected pioneer in sexual addiction studies, notes three levels of sexual addiction, with porn being at level one. If left uncontrolled, it can lead to level two behavior, which is illegal (exhibitionism, voyeurism, prostitution, unwanted touching, etc.), and then some purveyors progress to level three, which involves even more serious legal violations (rape, child molestations, and child pornography). Many people can look at porn occasionally and not reach a level-two offense, but the more someone looks at it, the more likely he is to drift in that direction.

If you are dating a guy who has an extensive past of watching porn and either can't stop or sees no reason to, you ought to be concerned for a couple of different reasons. One, his expectations surrounding what women do, enjoy, and how they act have been jettisoned to a dangerous place that bears zero resemblance to reality. In the world of internet sex, there is no "soul connection" depicted, which is the only real sexual connection that truly satisfies long-term. Internet sites create continued interest though shock value instead of intimacy. Rather than leading you to bond with someone who is familiar (God's intention for sex), they make you obsess about seeing something *new*, something *different*, every time, something even more whacked-out than what you saw last time. And thus the spiral toward more deviant forms of sexual expression continues.

The way porn works, a man's brain gets a dopamine hit every time he sees a different naked woman. But it has to be *new*. Few guys keep watching the same video or photo; familiarity means the video stops "working." All this ties sexual excitement to new and previously unseen sexual images. This is the exact opposite of marriage, where we are called to get sexually excited with a marriage partner we have seen naked hundreds or even thousands of times. Porn trains you to *not* find marital sex to be satisfying.

Listen, *healthy* marital sex is extremely pleasurable in every sense of the word. You don't have to try weird things to make it pleasant and keep it exciting. Two people who are connected relationally, emotionally, and spiritually, with bodies that function the way God made them to function, can have tremendously satisfying sex without resorting to unnatural or demeaning acts. The Bible gives marvelous freedom to a husband and wife to enjoy and pleasure each other in many creative and exciting ways.

So what do you do if you've already fallen for a guy with extensive pornography use in his past? What do you need to know if you decide to proceed? The mind of a guy steeped in pornography needs newer and perhaps kinkier thoughts and acts to reach the same level of excitement. Contemplating fifty to sixty *years* of sexual activity with such a mind should make you cautious. Furthermore, his soul has been selfishly shaped to be all about his pleasure. The whole concept of sex as a gift to be given is damaged. His thoughts will be, *Am I getting any tonight?* Women who sleep with guys like this tell me they feel "hunted," "used," and even "treated like a masturbatory website." That gets really old really fast.

On a spiritual and neurological level, guys who have a long history with pornography and multiple sexual partners are less able to bond with one woman sexually. They've trained their brains to connect sex with *women in general*, not *one woman in particular*. One of the prime purposes of sex—re-cementing marital affection—is compromised.

After hearing me speak on sex at a marriage conference, a young man in his twenties married to an attractive young woman of the same age confessed to me that, all things being equal, he actually preferred masturbating with pornography over having sexual relations with his wife. He was ashamed of this, he hated that this was so, but giving in so many times had made him actually prefer fake, imaginary sex over intimate relational sex. He hoped marriage would "cure" his problem, but all it did was expose it.

And guys, what do *you* need to know if you've fallen for a girl with extensive pornography use in her past? Debra Fileta has worked with many women who have fallen in this way:

> "First and foremost, you need to understand that your past doesn't define you, but it does influence you. Moving away from the negative effects of porn in someone's life requires time and intention.
>
> "You have to understand that love and affection for her won't bring long-lasting freedom, freedom is something she has to find standing alone. A couple questions to ask as you contemplate moving

forward: *How severe was the addiction?* The more
severe, the more difficult it will be to break free
once and for all. *How long ago was the addiction?* If
we're talking last week, you'd better put those brakes
on quickly. Healing from addictions doesn't happen
overnight, because addictions don't develop overnight. It takes time to build roots, and even more
time to dig them up. Before moving forward in a
relationship, it's important to see *at least* 6 months
of freedom from the influence of porn."[4]

The science of neuroplasticity is both a warning and a hope.
Neuroplasticity refers to the way our decisions literally (even
physiologically) shape our brains. We cultivate desires, habits, and
addictions. Repeated actions, over time, make us who we are. That's
the danger: what we *do* becomes a part of who we *are*, making us
more likely to do it again.

But neuroplasticity also means we can grow out of destructive
patterns. It's a slow process, but with education, counseling, accountability, and God's power within us, we can become new people who
make healthier choices day by day.

Restoration isn't built on the back of fraud and denial, however.
God heals through the practice of confession, repentance, and the
applied blood of Jesus Christ. Anything less won't cut it. But even
after forgiveness, the brain still often struggles to let go of the patterns
of the past. Forgiveness is one thing; sanctification (walking in holiness) is often something very different. Even after someone is forgiven,
his or her brain will need time to be rewired in a healthy direction.

Which is why, if you're a man or woman with a significant
history with pornography (to the extent that you've tried to stop

watching it and always fail), seek professional-level healing *now*. After a certain amount of time, pornography use ceases to be a moral issue and becomes a neurological one, so seek a counselor who knows what he or she is doing. It's worth the cost and potential embarrassment to be set free.

A sexually fulfilling marriage is priceless, and there is hope. Dealing with your past to make that possible is one of the best investments you'll ever make. Don't let Satan steal a lifetime of satisfaction from you by believing his lie that because of your past, you don't deserve sexual fulfillment in the future. This has nothing to do with what you *deserve*. It has everything to do with what Jesus *bought* on your behalf.

Here's even more hope: as a pastor, some of the strongest marriages I know are ones in which the guy has a past with pornography, has gone through a twelve-step group, and keeps working on recovery. Guys willing to do this introspective work often experience a special level of intimacy in marriage. They become more self-aware and more thoughtful relationally. It makes me wonder if everyone should go through some kind of recovery treatment, as these programs seem to address many relational issues in a positive way. (I'm sure this is likely true of women as well, but I haven't personally worked with any women in this situation.)

To be safe, you want to see your partner have at least six months of victory over this sin, without having sex with you to hold him up. Then you'll know he has the strength to stand firm when temptation strikes after marriage, because it will. If he has a history with it, he will struggle, to some degree, for years to come.

Rushing into marriage could be risky because some men, when they become infatuated, will stop looking at pornography for about a year, but when the infatuation fades, they'll go back to it. I'm not speaking as a trained psychologist who can explain this but rather drawing conclusions from anecdotal confessions. Several men have told me that the early days of marriage and sexual activity with their wives kept the porn compulsion away for just less than a year or so. When sex became routine, the old urges returned, and instead of working on their marital sexuality to make it more fulfilling, they found it easier to fall back into old patterns of self-pleasuring.

Which means, women, if you become sexually active with your boyfriend before he's your husband and he's had a long history with pornography, you don't know how true his healing really was. He might say, "I haven't looked at it since we've met," but how do you know that in another few months, once sex with you becomes a little more routine, he won't go right back to it? If you become sexually active and marry him within less than a year of meeting him, you're *hoping* that he really is healed, that he won't go back. A significant percentage of wives experience PTSD when they find out their husbands have been looking at porn, so the feelings of hurt and betrayal are deep and real.

Keep in mind: just because God designed sex to be pleasurable doesn't mean it's easy. You will have some issues to deal with to build a mutually satisfying sexual relationship. You don't want to be married to someone who will take a lazy shortcut to avoid having to work on a real relationship. If a guy's only sexual outlet is his wife, he'll be more inclined to work on the issues as they come up rather than ignore them.

A Promiscuous Past

You don't just marry a man or a woman; in a sense, you marry his or her past. Because of neuroplasticity, the more of a past there is, the more will need to be overcome.

Dr. Steve Wilke has been a therapist in California for over three decades. He has counseled many women who once posed for centerfolds for popular men's magazines as well as some former strippers. These women often had difficulty achieving sexual satisfaction. Though they seemed experienced in sexuality per se, they had almost no understanding of God-ordained sexual intimacy within marriage. Their prior connections with sex were about power and money. When sexual intimacy was supposed to be all about building intimacy with a man they truly cared about, the road to true relationship was very difficult to find. As a result, a lot of spiritual and psychological healing had to be accomplished in order for them to enter into a mutually satisfying relationship. They had to "unlearn" former patterns of psychological survival—playacting, hiding, and manipulating—and embrace the sometimes-scary marital realities of vulnerability and connection.

But here's the good news. Dr. Wilke has seen numerous couples healed of all kinds of sexual pasts to enjoy immensely fulfilling sexual relationships in marriage, to the extent that the sexual pasts don't even compare to sex in marriage.

Dr. Wilke explains the difference to his clients this way. "Before, sex was always about money, your own pleasure, power, or manipulation. Neither of you has ever surrendered yourselves in a relationship where you are truly loved, cared for, and protected, and where there is spiritual covering through prayer and the Word. You've never known Song of Songs or Garden of Eden sex. This will be the first time that you have ever experienced sex in the context that God created for both of you to enjoy. You have no idea how different this kind of sex will be."

To be fair to couples in these circumstances, Dr. Wilke suggests that getting there requires a tremendous amount of spiritual and psychological clinical work to replace old habits with new ones.

Potential mates with clinical backgrounds and histories should prepare for marriage with a trusted professional to learn to love in God-honoring ways. You might think that meeting with a professional sounds extreme, but if your past is complicated, it takes expertise. If you break an arm or tear a ligament, you need more than a cast—you also need physical therapy. The same principle applies spiritually. Once the damage is addressed and "fixed," you still need psychological and spiritual exercises to regain full health.

If a woman knows she is forgiven, understands the grace of God, and is loved by a man who is spiritually, relationally, and emotionally in tune with her, she will usually melt in his arms. Her past won't vandalize her future. The one exception is if there has been a moment or moments of severe sexual trauma—that takes a little more therapy.

And a guy who has repented of seeing women as conquests, or perhaps has had to get over being abused by an older relative, can finally see sex as a mutually pleasurable experience that brings healing and comfort rather than alienation, shame, and pain.

Which means, couples, that if either of you has a past that still causes you to wince, you need to seek the best counsel money can buy before you enter into marriage. When it comes to psychological health, most of us don't know what we don't know; the past keeps hindering our present pleasure, but we don't realize it or we don't know how to stop it. Because of Christ, however, and the Christian truths of forgiveness and redemption, if you honestly face your past, healthy sexual enjoyment is a realistic expectation for your marriage.

It comes down to this, for both men and women: past sexual sin has consequences that often must be overcome, even after forgiveness. If the person you're thinking of marrying has dealt or is dealing with his or her past in a healthy, mature, and gospel-centered manner, you can proceed with some degree of confidence. If you catch your intended lying to you, falling back into the same old unhealthy patterns, or refusing to do the mental, spiritual, and physical work necessary to be fully healed (such as seeking counseling or faithfully attending recovery group meetings), the marriage bed may eventually become one of your least favorite places on this earth.

A Sacred Trust

One of the things I love about marriage is how God calls two broken people together and secures a covenant relationship that supplies the necessary stability for them to heal and grow (seeking righteousness). You need to count the cost, however, in determining how much healing your future spouse needs. Before you get married, it's essential to discuss your sexual past—not in overly vivid detail, but with enough disclosure to give each other an honest appraisal of the issues you'll be facing after marriage. Let me put it this way: if I got married concealing a $100,000 debt, a serious health issue, or a prior felony that made future employment problematic, I would clearly be committing an act of fraud. In the same way, a future spouse deserves to know how much effort it's going to take to participate in a healthy, God-honoring sexual relationship with you.

Amy had a previous boyfriend break up with her because, he said, her sexual past was "too much for him to handle." Now married, Amy said, "At the time I thought his assertion was a horrible denial of God's grace, and I ridiculed him for it (privately). Now I see it as God's provision for me. Tyrell doesn't feel burdened by my past, and I don't feel burdened by his. We have been honest about it, and we both feel ready to embrace one another's shortcomings, whatever that means. We're committed to 'walk it out' with each other to wholeness and healing."

If, after sufficient exposure to your intended's past, you believe the person is healed and healing, it's not unwise to marry him or her. Once you make that decision, however, if you want to be a redemptive force in that person's life and experience Song of Songs sex, *you must let his or her past go.* One man received wonderful advice from his dad. After his girlfriend confessed her premarital promiscuity, the young man's dad told him, quite wisely, "You need to settle in your heart that you will *never*—whether it's in the heat of an argument or under any circumstances—use her past as a weapon."

An analogy: it is kind and generous to take on someone's debt when he or she becomes your spouse. But it would be cruel and petty to keep reminding that person after the wedding what you could have bought if only he or she hadn't accrued such debt. You don't have to take on someone's debt, but if you do, don't use it to demean or shame that person. In the same way, it can be kind and generous to marry a person with a more "complicated past" than you have. But if you do marry that person, you will undercut the security, intimacy, and stability of your marriage by *ever* using it as a weapon.

Sex is a powerful tool. In a healthy marriage, used appropriately, it can be nothing short of glorious. As people who believe God is the Creator of our bodies and our sexuality, we should be eager to embrace His good handiwork. But know this: the more powerful the tool, the more training and caution you need when learning to use it. That's what this chapter is all about—not scaring you away from sex but helping you to take sex further than perhaps you ever could have dreamed, as a servant of your intimacy, a protector of your purity, a renewer of your relationship, and a very sacred place of pleasure.

Searching Questions

1. Were you aware of the way sex affects us chemically and relationally? How should this knowledge affect the way you view premarital sex?

2. Why do you think the stereotype is that a couple is enthusiastically active sexually before the wedding but then sex becomes boring just months into the marriage? Can this decline be avoided? What can you do now, as a single, to not fall into that trap?

3. Consider the statement: "Any way you look at it, sexual involvement before marriage is unhelpful." Do you agree or disagree? Why?

4. Is it possible for a couple to know they are "sexually compatible" without having sex? Does this matter?

5. How important do you believe it is to know each other's sexual pasts? To what detail?

6. What are some wise steps a person can take to evaluate his or her partner's past? What, in your mind, constitutes a "particularly troubled past"? How can you determine whether a person is healed from his or her sexual past—whether sexual promiscuity, pornography, or abuse?

16

Problem People

I'm hoping that by now you've caught the vision for a marriage that seeks first the kingdom of God. As you're looking for a partner in that mission, you need to be on the lookout for personality traits that will undermine such a focus. Certain personality weaknesses might undermine marital satisfaction in general, but four specific traits make a *spiritually prosperous* marriage more difficult and should be avoided when choosing someone to marry: people who are takers, people you can't respect, "incomplete" people who aren't secure in their relationship with God, and indecisive people.

People Who Take

You can divide the world into two groups of people: those who derive great joy from giving, and those who derive their highest joy from taking. When a giver starts dating a taker, the danger is that they both get to do what they love most: the giver gets to give, and the taker gets to take, take, take, and both seem so happy. For a spiritually fruitful marriage, however, and for the sake of your children—not to mention the reality that eventually even givers need to learn how to receive—it's most beneficial to the kingdom of God to make sure the person you marry is a giver.

This isn't selfish; two givers geometrically increase their ability to give. They inspire each other to give more, and they release each other to give outside the relationship, thus multiplying the relationship's fruitfulness. Takers want to receive; they may even resent your focus being put on anyone but them and thus may undercut your ability to give by half. A giver married to a taker gets depleted and tired, which is why you want to find someone who knows how to love and give. Such an ideal isn't selfish; it's wise. If you marry a taker, you'll compromise your own ability to love others outside the marriage.

Marriage is a long journey during which both spouses must learn to give sacrificially and at times unilaterally. For instance, if a giver gets really sick or is laid off, even though he or she provided the bulk of the income, can the taker learn to give? In most cases, sadly, the answer is no. Instead of displaying empathy, takers often just feel sorry for themselves, abandon the relationship, or run around in an emotional/relational panic, adding to the giver's problems rather than addressing them.

If you marry a taker, you're sitting on a relational time bomb because you're making the bet that, as a giver, your fallen body and your fallen soul won't ever get *so* fallen that you'll someday need help, at least for a season. That's foolish, because you will.

I once spoke to a couple in which the husband had been a drug addict for ten years—their entire marriage. His wife had been outstanding in her care and patience. He finally submitted to God, was going through recovery, and asked me how "this *Sacred Marriage* stuff" might apply to him. I responded, "You have a great opportunity to begin giving back to your wife and serving her in a way you never have. She has put up with your addiction for a decade; now you can focus on serving her as part of your own healing, loving her as God's daughter, and asking God every day how you can love her like she's never been loved before."

"But wouldn't that be making her an idol?" he asked in all seriousness.

His wife had demonstrated heroic patience and love toward him for *ten years*, and he thought giving a little back to her now might be *idolatry*? Instead, he wanted practical ideas for his wife to help *him* succeed in recovery!

That's how extreme some takers can be. When a wife is giving birth to a child or suffering an illness, a taker's buddies hear only about how he's not getting any sex. When a husband who is the sole wage earner comes home, fixes dinner, takes care of the kids, and even cleans up the dishes, the taker wife thinks he's being selfish if he wants his twice-a-week bout of sexual intimacy (this is a real-life example, by the way), because she's tired from her tennis match.

Even if you're a giver who likes to give, it's exhausting being married to a taker. A taker will suck the life out of you in many ways, and in one sense undercut your ability to minister to others. You can still minister, but you'll have less energy to do so because your marriage will be holding you back.

If God is calling you to a ministry outside the home, don't even think about marrying a taker. Part of being a good steward toward a ministry call is building a life that can support that call, and marrying a taker will undercut that. I have told some singles, as they have described the dynamics of their dating relationship, "If you marry this person, he or she will become your primary ministry. You won't have much left over after taking care of this one person. Is this what you think God is calling you to?"

Am I Dating a Taker?

A taker's response is always, first and foremost, about him or her. Even when something bad happens to you, instead of showing empathy and offering help, takers turn it around to make it an inconvenience for them. They're taking a bad situation and making it worse.

An example is if you get delayed by a small fender-bender on the way to a date at a restaurant; when you finally get hold of your partner, a taker's first words are, "Why didn't you call sooner?" or, "So when can you get here? I feel like an idiot sitting here by myself." A giver would be more concerned about your comfort: "Don't stress; these things happen. What can I do to help you now? Do you need to be picked up? Can I make a call for you?" Givers' thoughts will be about helping *you*, not about how something you didn't plan is negatively affecting *them*.

Another mark of takers is that they will give when asked to but almost always ask for something in return. Remember, they derive satisfaction from what they receive, not what they give, so when they know they "should" give, they still try to get something in return. For example, if you say, "I really miss seeing my parents. Do you think we could drive down next weekend and pay them a visit?" A taker might agree but then treat it like a transaction where you have to "pay him back": "Sure, I'll do that, as long as you ..." A giver delights in giving because it gives delight to his beloved. A taker negotiates for the best deal.

A third thing to notice is that *givers give to many others*. Because givers truly receive joy in giving, they are generous with their parents, siblings, strangers, servers at restaurants, members at church, and so on. If your partner is generous only with you, she may be giving only to get something (i.e., your hand in marriage). Once your partner has that, the giving stops. Ask yourself, Does she derive joy from being used by God to bless others? Or does she seemingly resent every time she has to do anything for anyone else? If so, the time will come when your intended will resent having to do anything for *you*.

If it still sounds selfish to you to want to marry a giver, ask yourself the following questions: Do you want your kids to be raised by someone who will constantly be annoyed, or by someone who will parent with a servant's heart? Do you want to invite someone to a home where your spouse is more concerned about the floors or furniture getting dirty or where the guests feel welcomed? Do you want to sit in a restaurant with a date who treats the server like an underling or like a person who may need to be encouraged and prayed for?

The person you marry will be married to you in every facet of life. You're not just choosing a spouse—you're choosing a partner who will represent you, as half of a couple, to the rest of the world. Wouldn't you rather be part of a giving couple? Think about how much more you can give, how you can accelerate your family's ability to love others, when you join one giving heart to another.

Ask yourself, When you spend time with your partner, do you feel drained or invigorated? Would you describe the relationship as healing and supportive or exhausting and combative? To you givers, asking these questions may feel uncomfortable, but here's where I want you to consider marriage as a base to seek first the kingdom of God. When you know that someone has your back and will help you out if you get into trouble, that the spouse waiting for you at home won't be as frustrated by your delay as she will be delighted that God is using you, that he will want to listen to what happened and help you recover, you're freer to serve others.

Finally, what I'm about to say might seem, on the surface, somewhat contradictory to all I've said before, but it's an important qualification. A true giver can, and should, also receive. I need to give; to be healthy and to honor God, I need to serve my spouse. If my spouse won't let me serve her, I can't honor God or love her as I should. It's not healthy for a relationship to become one-sided. Givers who can't receive are actually being a bit prideful and selfish. Receiving my love and service is actually an act of love.

Jesus let His feet be washed. Jesus let His body be anointed with oil. Jesus let women support Him financially. Jesus received Mary's worship and receives ours. Jesus let Martha fix His meal. Jesus let Simon help carry His cross. Jesus is the greatest servant who ever lived, yet part of His servant nature was seen in His allowing others to serve *Him*.

The three laws of marital choice for a ministry-minded marriage should be character, character, and character.

People of Low Respect

As soon as you marry someone, you are biblically responsible to respect that person as your husband (1 Peter 3:1) or wife (v. 7). This will be much easier for you to follow if you marry someone who is respectable. Psychological studies mirror Scripture in this insight: people are happiest and most satisfied in their marriage when they are married to someone for whom they have a high level of respect. This is particularly true for kingdom-centered marriages.

If the person you are attracted to is not generally respected by people you trust and believe in, that's a real problem. While you can choose to respect someone just because he or she is your spouse, the kind of respect we're talking about is a respect engendered from a person's character and actions, not position. If you're embarrassed by this person, if you constantly have to reassure your friends and family that "what he or she did (or said) might look bad, but it's not as bad as you think," you're setting yourself up for a frustrating marriage. Racism, prejudice, dishonesty, laziness, gluttony, materialism, selfishness—all these grow *more* unpleasant the longer you have to accommodate them. If you're already tired of having to excuse your partner of one (or certainly several) of these, you're going to have a tough time when it comes to marital satisfaction twenty years from now.

Besides, if you have to mop up after her for how she alienates people, how he neglects people or displays boorish behavior, how are you going to support or, even more difficult, join his or her ministry? You'll be so busy trying to clean up and apologize for the mess your spouse has made that you won't have time left over to break new ground together.

The three laws of real estate are location, location, and location. The three laws of marital choice for a ministry-minded marriage should be character, character, and character.

Incomplete People

If someone thinks getting married is the cure for being lonely, purposeless, or friendless, he or she is being very foolish—and you're being just as foolish marrying that person. *Marriage doesn't solve emptiness; it exposes it*, so marry someone who has a solid core. If someone can't live without you, he or she will never be happy living with you either.

In *Loving Him Well*, my book for wives, I spent a good bit of time reminding wives that "God, not your marital status, defines your life." The reason I said this is that spiritual security is an essential platform for the full expression of biblical love. If I'm not secure in my relationship with God—that I am accepted, loved, and empowered by Him—then I won't risk saying something or doing something that might make my spouse angry or frustrated. That's a huge problem if your view of marriage is two sinful people walking a journey toward increased holiness.

When I know I'm loved by Christ, I can bear others' disapproval. When I know God accepts me, I can act in a way I'm convinced is right, even if it angers my family or my in-laws, so I'm free to serve my wife first over them. When I am secure in God's approval, I won't become a child-centered spouse, neglecting my wife in a desperate search to make my kids appreciate me, because that need for acceptance will already have been met by God. I will be free to love and train my kids while still keeping my wife as my top priority.

Marrying a person who feels complete in Christ will help you pursue Christ's call to righteousness in Matthew 6:33 by giving you a partner in holiness. If I'm acting like a jerk at a restaurant, I want a wife who will call me out on it before I alienate all my friends. If you're a mom who is alienating her son, don't you want a husband who will confront you respectfully so that you can grow your relationship with your boy instead of losing him?

It takes a secure man or woman to stand up to a spouse. The Bible tells us we are more than capable of being deceived by our sin, so why wouldn't we want to be married to someone who can effectively counteract that rather than go along with it because he or she is too insecure to speak up?

Self-respect is a necessary ingredient for being in a successful partnership. Men and women who can't stand on their own in Christ will be limited in what they can contribute to a marriage.

Indecisive People

What if someone has read up to this point in the book, believes he or she has found someone who wants to base a family on Matthew 6:33, who has complementary marriage style expectations, who is a giver and a person of respect, and who is rooted in God—but this particular reader still can't make up his or her mind, even after a couple of years of dating. Is that a problem?

It might be.

Some believers say they must wait for a "sign from God" before they feel "released" to marry. This book has challenged the claim that there is only one person to marry. We've demonstrated, scripturally, that the choice is up to you—both whether to get married and whom you should marry. Since that's the clear biblical teaching, if your partner insists on an additional "divine sign," that's a good indication that your potential spouse likely lacks necessary confidence and the ability to make decisions. A good chunk of life is about making decisions: where to work, where to buy a house, when to have kids, whether to take a job, who to make friends with, and the like.

There's a personal element to this as well. If I had been dating someone for two years and she still wasn't "sure" she wanted to marry me unless God made something miraculous happen to confirm her decision, I'd feel more than a little slighted! I'd want her—based on character, compatibility, life goals, and personality—to be *eager* to marry me. Don't disrespect who you are by allowing someone to string you along and use God's failure to offer a miraculous sign as an excuse to keep putting off the proposal.

Remember, if there's not just one person to marry, you can courageously move on to find someone else who is more suitable for you. When you find and then choose someone who is growing in the ability (and confidence) to make wise decisions—including the decision to marry you—you're well on your way to building a God-honoring family.

Searching Questions

1. Gary stated that some people are takers and some people are givers, but isn't this a matter of degree? How can you tell if someone is primarily in one camp or the other?

2. How might accepting Jesus' words to "seek first the kingdom of God" affect your concern over whether the person you are marrying is a taker? Does this make such an evaluation more or less important? How so?

3. Do you ever find it hard to receive from others? How might refusing to do so sometimes be selfish?

4. Why do you think that when people feel "in love" they are willing to stay with a partner for whom they have little or no respect? What can we do to guard against this?

5. What would likely be some common problems if you married someone who wasn't secure in who she is, who felt like he needed someone else to complete him?

6. Would someone insisting on a sign from God before he or she gets married make you more or less interested in that person? Why? What do you think the Bible has to say about this?

How Would Jesus Date?

So far I've been encouraging you to put your intended through the spiritual equivalent of an SAT test. Now it's time to ask, What about you? Are you dating with integrity? In your pursuit of a good marital match, are you acting with grace and kindness? Is the *process* of your search honoring God?

In the interest of full disclosure, I did a miserable job of this as a single, so I can't use myself as an example. I was too quick to enter into exclusive relationships and often just as quick to get out. Emotionally, it was difficult for me to go any significant period of time without having a girlfriend, so I almost always had one.

Fortunately, we have a much more reliable source to turn to: Jesus. While Jesus never dated, He did have friends, and His friendships reveal the nature of His relationships in such a way that we can imagine how He would date.

John 11 is a great case in point. Jesus built a strong friendship with Mary, Martha, and Lazarus. When Lazarus grew very sick, the sisters sent word to the miracle-working rabbi to hurry back to Bethany because Jesus' friend was close to death. Remember, doctors were all but useless then. Jesus was their *only* hope. Yet Jesus purposefully delayed His visit until after Lazarus's death.

It looked very bad on the surface. The Jews in Bethany had tried to kill Jesus, so Martha and Mary knew they were asking Jesus to risk His life to return. An uncharitable view of His delay might have been that Jesus was afraid. A slightly less uncharitable view might have been that Jesus was just too busy or indifferent to a close friend's need. Grief isn't always rational, and the accusations that later flew out of these women's mouths when Jesus did show up demonstrated their distrust.

As God, Jesus knew His friends would feel betrayed. Even so, in the words of classical writer R. Somerset Ward, "He disciplined the natural impulse of his affection and waited."[1] Ward's language gets a bit archaic here, so let me paraphrase the rest: Jesus' friendship was so true that He put His actions above what His friends would think about His actions. He knew they would question Him, but He did what He knew was right anyway.

Is your friendship great enough to put your loved one's good above your loved one's opinion of you? That's a difficult place to get to, but it's the only foundation for mature love. You have to become the kind of person who does what's best even if the person you love doesn't think you're acting with the proper motive or concern.

According to Ward, such "unselfishness is only possible by means of discipline, of warfare with selfish desires. The highest bond of friendship is forged in the fire of discipline, and it is true to experience to say that the greater the cost of the forging, the greater will be the friendship."[2]

Most people think the highest bond of friendship is the fire of emotion and affection. What makes someone a friend in the modern mind is that we *like* or feel fondly toward that person. Ward suggested, and Jesus modeled, that the highest bond of friendship is personal discipline. Friendship is doing what's best for someone, even if what's best is confusing or feared or resented. To get to this place, we literally have to declare spiritual war against our selfishness.

Is your friendship great enough to put your loved one's good above your loved one's opinion of you?

Romance is built on loud and unreserved displays of lavish affection, but such displays can be evidence of an undisciplined heart. Sometimes the most loving thing to do is to limit your displays of affection by submitting to God's greater good for this person. Jesus could have immediately traveled to Lazarus and healed him—and never given Mary or Martha an opportunity to question His love—or He could have allowed Lazarus to die, allowed Mary and Martha to go through a natural questioning of His love and commitment, and thereby teach them a valuable spiritual lesson. Jesus chose the spiritual lesson and waited until Lazarus died.

It goes a little deeper than this, however. Jesus told His disciples that more than pleasing Mary and Martha and even saving Lazarus was at stake: it was God's will for Jesus to raise Lazarus from the dead. Jesus couldn't do that unless He first let Lazarus die. Jesus lived first and foremost for the glory of God, above every human friendship, and that made Him the truest friend any man or woman could ever have.

Jesus' decision to return to Bethany shows the courage of His friendship. Circumstances looked so bleak that His disciples thought He was committing Himself to certain death. The disciple Thomas said to the other disciples, "Let us also go, that we may die with him" (John 11:16). Jesus wasn't moved by the opinion of His friends or the threat of His enemies; He lived entirely to fulfill the will of God.

A Deliberate Man

Notice how deliberately and purposefully Jesus acted in friendship, without regard to His safety or reputation. Let me ask you a tough question: When you see a friendship or romance just beginning to bloom, are you deliberate or impatient? Do you seek God's face before you "explore" your feelings and discuss them? If your feelings are contrary to God's will, they are, at that moment, irrelevant, if indeed Jesus is your God and not just your "friend."

Many couples tend to be undisciplined and hasty in declaring their affection. They rush in and blurt out their feelings before seriously even knowing the other person. And then they tend to be very self-centered, wanting the other person to respond in kind and begin meeting their romantic fantasies with equal desperation.

Jesus does the exact opposite. Ward pointed out that the mistake we often make in our friendships is that we "give too generously what is useless to our friend"—that is, easy displays of affection— and then we are too stingy in giving the "more costly gifts"—that is, sacrificially reining in our feelings until we know we can back them up. He continued, "At the back of all appearances lies the truth that the measure of love is its costliness. To analyze one's feelings is the worst way of arriving at a measure of friendship; to count its cost is the best way."[3]

To analyze one's feelings is the worst way of arriving at a measure of friendship; to count its cost is the best way.

Jesus lived and taught that friendship and love are marked by sacrifice: "Greater love has no one than this: to lay down one's life for one's friends" (John 15:13). Feeling romantically inclined toward someone but not mentioning it because you know doing so would be premature and unwise is one of the most loving and difficult things you will ever be asked to do. It is difficult to feel so strongly and not talk about it with the one you're infatuated with. And it is so delicious to hear that the feelings are returned. But giving free rein to such emotion and conversation can be the opposite of love; it may be selfish. It threatens that person's emotional and spiritual health. It shows a lack of concern, a lack of care, a total lack of the willingness to sacrifice on which true love is based.

Displays of public affection, verbal commitments that are born out of sheer emotion, false promises based on temporary emotions—these are the "useless" gifts that Ward says we can be so generous with. But then we're too stingy with the costly gifts essential for the other person's well-being: we don't consider his or her welfare before we pronounce our commitment or affection; we don't consider whether our displays of affection will be healthy or cause possible confusion and later hurt. Are you learning to deny your selfish desires and put the other person's spiritual welfare ahead of your own emotional and physical desires?

How do you truly know whether you are committed to this person and that you truly love him or her? Here's how you know: analyzing your feelings is the "worst way of arriving at a measure of friendship; to count the cost is the best way." Your love is measured by your willingness to act unselfishly, to even let the person think less of you, if in doing so you are serving his or her spiritual advancement. If you would rather *not* declare your love because you want to make sure the relationship is wise, that's counting the cost. That's love. If you would rather know whether your feelings are returned before you even know whether the relationship would honor God, that's selfishness. Analyzing your feelings is a waste of time (though that's what many singles focus on). Analyze instead the fruit of love, your willingness to sacrifice, and your commitment to the other person's welfare.

That's what Jesus did with Mary and Martha. According to Ward,

> In our Lord's mind we can see that the *spiritual* welfare of the household at Bethany was the first consideration. The wait of two days was doubtless to enable them to understand more fully their loss, and to draw out more completely their faith. The tie which bound our Lord to them was knit most closely with their souls. If we would be true friends, giving ourselves to those we love, we must put the spiritual before the material in our relationship with them. Marriage or friendship, which is not based on some mutual spiritual outlook and ideal, can never reach perfection.[4]

A God-honoring friendship is one of the best realities of life. A friendship that might also lead to marriage is even more exciting, which is all the more reason we should guard it and make sure it is built on a solid foundation:

> The spirit in which we enter on a friendship, determines its growth. Too often we enter lightly and without thought into friendship, but if we consider it as a part of spiritual life, we shall be saved from

> this disaster. In such a case we shall approach it as a
> serious matter, striving to discipline it rightly from
> the start, prepared to give our best to it, however
> costly it may be, keeping it above the material in a
> spiritual sphere. If we can accomplish this by God's
> help our life will be enriched by the greatest gift to
> be found on earth, a friendship such as Christ gave
> to Lazarus and his sisters.[5]

Now, not only is this how you should treat others, but it is also how you should expect your future husband or wife to treat you. If your potential future spouse is generous with the things that don't really matter—physical displays of affection, cheap words of commitment based mostly on emotional intensity—but stingy with the things that do matter—disciplining his or her love so that it builds you up in the faith and leads you closer to God—then that person is not the right one for you.

Don't sell yourself short. If someone is pressuring you physically, that person is being selfish and destructive, even though the selfishness and destruction may be masked by passion. You need to be with someone who will honor you enough even to deny you what you ask for if he or she realizes that what you are asking for is not good for you spiritually.

I am so convicted writing this chapter. I *so* did not live this way as a single! If you've messed up, I completely understand. There's time now to do it differently going forward. Put the spiritual first, learn to love in a way that is truly love, and learn to date like Jesus would have dated. Doing so will help you make a wiser marital choice, and just as importantly, it will help forge the character you will need to have a spiritually intimate marriage.

Searching Questions

1. Why is it important when we seek to choose some-one to marry that the process honors God?

2. Why do think, given all they had already seen, that Mary and Martha were still inclined to doubt Jesus? What might this teach us about our own responses to God's work in our lives today?

3. How does the way people date, express their feelings, or make a commitment reflect on their character?

4. Describe how someone can practically apply these words: "To analyze one's feelings is the worst way of arriving at a measure of friendship; to count its cost is the best way."

Knowing When It's No

Never marry for mercy.

If, while reading this, you have serious concerns about proceeding with a relationship, your heart may begin to fight back: "I don't want to hurt him." "It would be so embarrassing to break things off now." "We've told everyone; I can't do that to her." "He's basically a good person, so I'm just going to go ahead with it."

These are understandable and even commendable sentiments, but they are disastrous conclusions. This is where the why of marriage is supremely important, and mercy, in this case, is a woefully unwise motivation.

A young woman asked me about dating a guy with a temper who was also young in his faith. She felt she was "dragging him along," spiritually speaking. "I care about him," she said, "and want the best for him."

"Good for you," I said, "but that doesn't mean you need to be in a romantic relationship with him or certainly not that you should *marry* him. Let me put it another way, especially since you're so young: Is he the *best* you can do? Is this the best man you can give to your future children as a dad? Are you confident that if you wait, you'll not find a man who is less angry and more spiritually mature?"

You have to be realistic. Given what you can bring to the marriage relationship, are you selling yourself—and your future children—short, or is this as good a match as you could hope to make? It's not selfish to want to make a wise marital choice. It is, in fact, foolish to make an unwise marital choice. If you go through with a less-than-wise marital choice, your future kids will suffer for the rest of their lives. You will suffer. Your community and church will suffer the consequences of a dysfunctional marriage. Your spouse will ultimately suffer, as who wants to be married to someone who regretted the marriage even before the wedding took place?

Most of us will get just one chance to build a family that seeks first God's kingdom. Wanting the best person to seek that kingdom with is being a good steward of your life. It's being kind to your future children. It's a gift to God's church. It's a powerful witness to the outside world. It's an act of love.

It is foolish to think the best way to avoid short-term pain—breaking up with someone—is by entering uncertainly into a lifetime relationship. If you know the relationship isn't wise or right, end it. At the very least, delay the wedding. Yes, it may be embarrassing. Yes, there will be tears and hurt feelings. But getting married to avoid short-term pain and embarrassment is like fleeing the country to become an exile for life just to avoid paying a twenty-five-dollar fine for jaywalking. You've lost all sense of proportion.

If you're wavering, ask someone to help you. Go to a parent, a counselor, a friend, or a pastor, and ask for his or her assistance: "I know I need to end it, but I don't know how. On my own, I won't. Please, don't let me go through with this. Help me to end it in the kindest way possible."

Any counselor or married person will
tell you that single and lonely is easier
to fix than married and lonely.

Mercy Marriages

"Marrying for mercy" means going through with a wedding even after problem areas have been exposed. There are many reasons people decide to proceed rather than postponing the wedding to make sure the relationship is solid or to work on issues.

Many times, these issues are related to ceremony logistics: losing deposit money for the hall, the availability of your dream church, or the cost of the wedding dress you've already purchased. This is short-term thinking, at best. In the course of your life, where you get married won't matter a millionth as much as who you're married to. The wedding ceremony will last, on average, thirty to forty minutes; your marriage will affect you for fifty or sixty years. Don't let something so short-term and trivial rush you into making such a long-lasting and profound commitment.

Another form of "marrying for mercy" is getting married because you had sex and think that now you have to. Letting an act of sin lead you into a lifetime of foolishness doesn't honor God. That's heaping sin upon sin in an attempt to make things right. No, you shouldn't have slept together, but going through with an unwise marital choice won't erase your sin—only the cross of Christ can do that. Don't condemn your kids to growing up in a less-than-mature home simply because, in a moment of passion, you gave yourself away when you shouldn't have. Marriage is about more than you. It's about your kids, your community, your church, the kingdom of God. Punishing yourself by going through with an unwise marriage because you've sinned is, first, blindness to God's grace and mercy; second, an offense against wisdom; and third, a potential act of cruelty toward your future children.

It's a lie for a couple to rationalize and say, "If we decide we're going to get married we can start having sex now, and God will consider us married," *and* it's a lie to suggest that one act of sexual intercourse *makes* you married. Otherwise, all those people who are "living in sin" by living together without getting married aren't really living in sin—they're actually married in God's eyes and the ceremony doesn't matter. Such thinking puts formulaic piety above wisdom and righteousness.

A third form of marrying for mercy is marrying someone because you feel sorry for that person, perhaps even thinking that no one else would marry him or her. Again, for the sake of the church, your future children, and the potential for you to live the most spiritually influential life possible, this is an act of poor stewardship. It's not your life, your body, your future to give away. We belong to God, first and foremost. We live to please Him before we live to please anyone else. If God calls you to marry someone, you need to be open to that, but make sure it's a genuine call, not an act of guilt or false mercy.

This is *not* to dissuade you from marrying a person who is seriously disabled, taking medicine for a mental illness, or dealing with some issues in his or her past that you know will be troublesome. These marriages, entered into wisely by discerning people with hearts in the right place, can supremely glorify God. There's no "perfect" person to marry! The motivation, however, must be companionship and biblical love, not feeling sorry for someone. Let a pastor or wise counselor grill you. Make sure your advisor is the kind of person who is strong enough to challenge you or release you before he or she blesses you. If the relationship is right and wise, it will stand up to the strongest scrutiny.

Finally, mercy marriages may include getting married because you feel sorry for *yourself,* so you compromise and agree to marry someone you know isn't a good match but is the best you can find right now and you just want to get the search over with. This is getting married because you want to be married rather than getting married because you've found a great match. Desperation and dating are a toxic mix.

Having friends who get engaged over the holidays—particularly if the friends have dated for less time than you have—can make you even more eager to tie the knot. That's why, interestingly enough, a lot of couples break up in January. So many of their friends got engaged that when this couple didn't, they think there must be something wrong with their relationship.

Resist this pressure to tie the knot just because others are rushing the process. If you make a subpar marital decision, you'll soon *increase* your agony and the pressure you live under, not relieve it. You'll face new pressure, new frustrations, new challenges—and all of them on a higher level.

Getting married to whomever you happen to be dating just because you're tired of being single is like buying a house because it's next to a restaurant and you just happen to be hungry. It might be convenient for that one meal, but do you want to eat there for the rest of your life?

Change for the sake of change rarely works out. Be focused in your pursuit, patient in your search, wise in your final deliberation.

Any counselor or married person will tell you that single and lonely is easier to fix than married and lonely. Don't take a bad situation and make it *worse*. As my good friend Ben Young says, getting married won't make you happy or an adult; getting married simply makes you … *married*.

More Bad Reasons to Get Married

In their book *The One*,[1] Ben Young and Samuel Adams give a few other bad reasons that people go through with a wedding.

"I've invested too much time and energy [in this relationship to let it go]."

This is an all-too-common sentiment, and its danger lies in seriously shortsighted thinking. Agreeing to be married to someone for fifty years because you've been in a frustrating relationship for five years makes no sense. At some point you must cut your losses. If you realize you made a foolish decision to get in the relationship and then made a second foolish decision to stay in the relationship too long, don't make a third catastrophic decision of cementing the relationship.

"I'm scared of what the person might do if [we break up]."

This can go two ways: you might be afraid that the person will hurt you or will hurt himself or herself. Either way shows the person's unsuitability as a marriage partner.

If you're scared to break up with someone because of what he or she might do to you, do you want to live in fear for the rest of your life? This is the time to get free, not to maintain the nightmare, and certainly not to create children who will share your nightmare. If you're afraid of angering this person, your children will also be afraid—do you really want to create a family with such a person? I'm not saying you should be rash in this situation. In fact, if you're truly scared, I urge you to work with a counselor who has experience handling abusive people so that you can learn the safest way to break out of the relationship. But break out of it you must.

If your concern is that the person might do harm to himself or herself, once again, ask yourself if you want to live for the rest of your life with the burden of having to keep someone happy or else watch that person resort to self-violence. This might sound harsh, but you need to hear it: it's never your fault if someone hurts himself or herself because you initiate a breakup, if you do so with integrity and compassion. You shouldn't be a jerk about the way you end the relationship, and you certainly shouldn't be cruel. You can expect the person to show emotion and even anger, but anything else is his or her problem, not yours. If that person's response is all out of whack, something has happened to him or her outside of and prior to your relationship that has led to such a rash response, and you are neither responsible for it nor capable of fixing it.

Of course, you'll want to be extra sensitive. I would recommend working with a counselor, alone, to plot out how to bring the relationship to an end in the kindest, cleanest way. If you do all that you can do to act with integrity, you should bear no guilt if someone else chooses to act inappropriately. Had you stayed with such a person, you would be *feeding* the illness, not curing it. Perhaps your leaving will be the wake-up call that person needs to seek help.

"God's called me to carry this cross."

Really? Has God also called your future children to carry that cross? Has God called someone else to whom you could have been happily married to also carry a cross, since he or she will be denied a lifetime with you?

I remember speaking with a divorced middle-aged woman who felt God was calling her into a significant ministry. She was dating a professional man who was economically and socially very successful but particularly young in his faith.

"If you marry this man," I warned her, "he'll become your ministry. You're not going to get much from him, and it's going to take a lot out of you to keep the family healthy. Also keep in mind that you'll be sabotaging this other ministry that you believe God may be calling you to. Are you sure this is God's will for you?"

When you accept a cross, you're limiting your ability to carry other crosses, so make doubly sure you know what you're doing. Because of the account of Hosea, I can't say God has never called anyone into a difficult marriage, but it's clear the Bible doesn't see the case of Hosea as normative.

Rowdy and Anna

My friends Byron and Carla Weathersbee have counseled numerous couples considering marriage. One story they tell in their book *Before Forever*[2] might seem sad, but it has a happy ending.

Rowdy and Anna met at a Young Life camp and fell deeply in love: "Long conversations while washing dishes led to one of those Hollywood-scripted moments together on the beach. You know the scene. As the sun set, they began to drop their guard in free-flowing conversation and found they had the same vision and passion for Christ. They laughed, they shared, they entered each other's worlds, matching dreams and lifestyle plans. And they both liked what they saw. It was at that moment that Rowdy just knew that this was the one!"

Rowdy transferred to Anna's university so they could be together and build the relationship, which eventually led Rowdy to pop the question. Even though Anna had told Rowdy (on more than one occasion) that he would need to ask her dad for his blessing before approaching her, Rowdy talked to Anna first. This turned what could have been a very romantic moment into a very frustrating one for Anna and a bewildering one for Rowdy.

They managed to overcome the awkwardness and still got engaged, but the incident itself became a picture of some significant differences in their personalities. Here's how Byron and Carla described it: "Rowdy plowed through life like an ice-breaker through frozen seas.... If Rowdy ever found himself in trouble, he used his charm and humor to wiggle out of it.... Rowdy was a bright, sharp-tongued, make-it-happen kind of guy who lived life in the fast lane."

Anna loved these traits about Rowdy and saw them in a positive light; her parents had a bit of a negative spin. They thought Rowdy could be "controlling, unkind, and sometimes verbally abusive." Then the Weathersbees uncovered in premarital counseling that Rowdy had some significant debt due to sports gambling (he called it "bad investments"). But, as for most couples, these sobering issues didn't shake either Anna's or Rowdy's confidence. Both thought, *If we could just get married, share life, and regain focus on our vision that we talked about that evening at Young Life camp, then some of those issues would resolve themselves—wouldn't they?*

See, that's what happens. After engagement, couples see issues and think that marriage will resolve them. You've already invested so much in the relationship—you've even gotten engaged!—that the thought of it not working out is too terrible to contemplate. So you just hope that marriage will make everything better.

But it got more troublesome in the case of Rowdy and Anna. When Anna left the Midwest, where she was raised, and moved to

New York to be near Rowdy, she was shocked at the reality of city life. She had grown up in the suburbs, "where the greatest dangers included staying out of the path of families out for an evening bike ride together." She soon had her fill of "all that noise, all those dirty, unkempt people, expensive rent for a nasty one-room apartment, and that hectic subway-chasing, taxi-hailing, look-no-one-in-the eyes lifestyle."

Quite wisely, Rowdy and Anna eventually realized that who Anna was and who Rowdy was didn't mix all that well. While they respected each other, were attracted to each other, and truly cared for each other, getting married wouldn't be the wisest thing to do.

I'm impressed at their character. Think about it: Rowdy had changed universities to build the relationship with Anna. Anna had defended Rowdy to her parents, and then, after college, moved to New York to be near Rowdy. They had spent some prime years together and even announced their engagement to their family and friends. They had invested *so much* that it would have been *so easy* to just go along with the marriage.

But they didn't. They broke up. It was sad. It was embarrassing. It was hurtful.

But here's how the story ends. Today, as Byron and Carla explain,

> Rowdy survives on the money he makes trading futures. Many days he loses big money—but he has also found that he does not need much to survive. He also works full time for a ministry that mentors inner-city kids after school in a rough, drug-saturated neighborhood. He loves the high risk and rewards that inner-city ministry and the stock market bring, as well as the uncertainty and

action that each day drops on him. He is fulfilling his passion to serve Christ in a radical way.

Anna is now married to a wonderful man and teaches in a suburban, Midwestern school near where she grew up. Out of the security that her husband and family bring to Anna, she ministers to high school girls who struggle with self-esteem issues and eating disorders.... She is passionate about Midwestern life and her relationship with Christ, and God has brought her a husband who shares similar passions.[3]

It was difficult breaking up, but the ending, as you can see, is very happy. Both Rowdy and Anna have spiritually rich and meaningful lives—just not with each other. They are both seeking first the kingdom of God, but they wisely realized that their respective roles in that kingdom weren't compatible. If you find yourself at an excruciatingly painful crossroads, as Rowdy and Anna did, try to remind yourself of this: when you close the door on a current bad relationship, you're not jumping off a cliff; you're just opening the door to another life.

Saying Good-Bye

If after seeking God's best for you, you determine it's time to part ways, here are some tested strategies and godly wisdom for bringing a relationship to an end.

SOONER IS BETTER THAN LATER

Once you know the relationship has run its course, don't prolong its inevitable end. Don't stay together simply because your girlfriend's sister is getting married in a month and you've already agreed to be at the wedding. I say this because more damage can be done and more hurt can be leveled in a month of uncertainty than in a year of trial and error. It's just human nature. Your girlfriend (or boyfriend) will sense you're pulling away, and when she brings it up and you deny it, she'll be able to rightfully accuse you of dishonesty and wasting her time.

I'm not saying you should run as soon as you have any hesitation; be deliberate and thoughtful. If you didn't enter a relationship too hastily, there's no reason to get out of it too hastily. But when you arrive at the point where you know there is no chance the relationship will progress toward marriage, be open, honest, and clear.

BE HELPFUL, BUT NOT A COUNSELOR

When your partner wants to know why you're breaking up, be honest. Compassionately but clearly state the main reasons. Keep in mind, however, that this isn't the time for counseling. If the issue is that the guy has no ambitions, say so: "I just don't see you going anywhere right now vocationally, and that's a huge problem for me." This helps him and chases away some of the uncertainty that creates even more hurt. But then don't get sucked into a counseling session where he might come back with, "Well, what if I send out more applications or take that internship? Do you think that would be wise?" At that point, be direct: "I'm not the one to discuss this with, and this isn't the time or place, because whatever you do, it's not going to change what's happening here."

Some people, by not giving any reasons, risk creating anger that takes a long time to resolve. You're trying to be nice by remaining silent, but the other person usually takes it the other way, feeling that it's cruel to leave him or her hanging—and that person has a point if the relationship has been a significant one. So if you can find a sensitive, tactful way to explain why you're breaking things off, do so. Giving that person some clues can help him or her grow through the experience, which is kind, but that doesn't mean you become a counselor and try to fix what went wrong.

OWN THE DECISION

Don't blame your parents, your friends, or God. You made the call to get into the relationship, and you should own the decision to break it off.

When you say, "God is leading me to end this" (particularly if the person is less spiritually mature than you are), you're risking making the person angry with God instead of you, when in reality you should be more concerned about how he or she is doing with God than how he or she feels about you.

Your desire not to pursue marriage is legitimate; in the end, that's all someone else needs to know. It's your decision. Own it.

IF IT'S OVER, SAY THAT IT'S OVER

Don't say "It's time to take a break" if you don't ever intend to get back together again. If the relationship is over for good, say so. It's unkind to leave a boyfriend or girlfriend hanging or to give false hope, just to spare you the pain of watching that person hurt. Hurt will come eventually, because one day he or she will realize you're never going to get back together again—either when you start dating someone else or when more time passes and you don't pursue your former partner. If you give any hope, that person may even expect you to let him or her know if you meet someone else, which will set up another painful conversation.

Do yourself and this person a favor: end it completely, thoroughly, and without any ambiguity.

The Highest Stakes Imaginable

Let me remind you that the stakes are simply too high to compromise on this: *never marry for mercy*. Get married because this is the best person you can find with whom you can live a life that will honor God. You only have one life, one body, one heart to give away. Make it count. The first step toward a wise, God-honoring, and fulfilling marriage is often ending an unwise, energy-sapping, misery-producing dating relationship.

Searching Questions

1. What are the benefits, to you and others, of you making a wise marital choice?

2. Have you ever spoken to someone who confessed that he (or she) got married even knowing he shouldn't have? What was his story? Why did he go through with the wedding?

3. Do you believe a couple becoming sexually active should get married just because they are sexually active? Why or why not?

4. What are the dangers of marrying someone in part because you feel sorry for that person? What are other poor reasons why people go through with weddings?

5. What do you think would have happened if Rowdy and Anna had gone through with the wedding? How can their story encourage other couples?

6. Of the following strategies for ending a relationship, are there any you disagree with? Any you would add?
   - Sooner Is Better Than Later
   - Be Helpful, but Not a Counselor
   - Own the Decision
   - If It's Over, Say That It's Over

A New Vision

When Adoniram Judson wrote to Ann Hasseltine's father, asking for Ann's hand in marriage, he didn't sugarcoat the future. Intent on becoming the first foreign missionary from the United States, Adoniram was up front about the dangers Mr. Hasseltine's daughter might face:

> I have now to ask whether you can consent to part with your daughter, whether you can consent to her departure to a heathen land, and her subjection to the hardships and suffering of a missionary life. Whether you can consent to her exposure to the dangers of the ocean, to the fatal influence of the southern climate of India, to every kind of want and distress, to degradation, insult, persecution, and perhaps a violent death.[1]

It's not like Ann lacked options. Widely considered "the most beautiful girl in Bradford, Massachusetts," Ann had more than her share of suitors. Yet it was Adoniram who gained her affection, and his letter to her father, sadly, proved prophetic. Once in Burma, the couple lost a child to tropical fever, and when war broke out,

Adoniram was arrested for being a spy. He hung upside down for days on end, suspended from the ceiling, while Ann desperately sought his release. She finally managed to visit her husband eight months after his arrest and handed over a precious bundle: newborn daughter Maria.

Months followed, and though Adoniram was finally released, both Ann and Maria died of fever soon thereafter.

The horrific events pushed Adoniram into a nervous breakdown, but he supernaturally persevered and went on to live a life overflowing with faithful spiritual labor.

God may not have called you to the mission field, but I want you to consider what brought Adoniram and Ann together: a mission so large that they willingly faced, and then endured, some of the worst nightmares imaginable.

Let me give you an even worse nightmare, however: a marriage without a mission, a life without purpose, a relationship without any end beyond its own "happiness." Matthew 6:33, seeking first the kingdom of God, will breathe life into any marriage and remains, I am convinced, the single best reason for two people to join their futures together. Such couples aren't lost in simply pursuing a pleasant five or six decades; they are determined to live a life with eternal impact.

Remember the tale of two tears—the two stories with which I began this book? One married person cried tears of frustration; the other was crying tears of joy. I asked, What kind of tears do you want to be shedding ten years from now?

Having been writing and speaking on marriage for two decades, I've seen how much time and effort are spent by people trying to survive and fix extremely difficult marriages. I don't think any marriage is easy. But some marriages really do require an extra amount of maintenance. If you marry an addict who won't work on recovery or someone who is spiritually immature, for instance, you're setting yourself up for a lifetime of distractions.

The apostle Paul said this is one of the main concerns when considering marriage. He pointed out that married people are distracted, having to spend significant time and mental effort to please their husbands or wives. However, some marriages are more distracting, while other marriages provide a base of support for more focused service to God.

I ended my book *Sacred Marriage* with the picture of "holy couples." We usually think of saints as individuals, but what if we took marriage seriously enough to talk about saintly couples, marriages where God is unusually present and active, to the extent where one new identity emerges, a family established on seeking first the kingdom of God?

> What if a few Christian couples took this pioneering challenge seriously, and set out to become a "couple saint"? No longer defining their relationship to God in solitary terms, but working together to present themselves as a holy unit, a pair of cherubim in the middle of whom God's presence is radically awakened?
>
> It is ... an interesting invitation. Is there anyone who will take up that invitation for today?[2]

If singles would consider this *before* they get married, if they would purify their motives to pursue marriage, and if they would make this the basis of whom they choose to marry, we'd see much more of this. In other words, if you look at the question of why you want to marry before you choose whom to marry, you're more likely to make a wiser choice about the who. It's not a choice between either why or who. It's that asking the why question first helps you choose the *best* who.

I ache for the day when people make such wise marital choices that they can pray through where to live to make the most significant impact for Christ instead of praying they could merely be able to exist in the same house without yelling and fighting. I pray that God will raise up couples who are so in tune with each other that they will be that much stronger to withstand the inevitable spiritual assaults that are unleashed on any productive Christian. I pray Christian believers will conceive and/or adopt a lot of children and let those kids see what a God-centered marriage looks like. I pray that while such couples will certainly need times of support and counsel on their own as they work through the issues of their sin, even more they will be a resource to other couples—of counsel, prayer, encouragement, and example.

Much kingdom time is wasted on ill-matched people trying to make their marriages a little less insufferable. I want you to gain a positive picture—a vision for how much kingdom work could be accomplished by two well-matched people working in harmony to seek the kingdom of God, grow in righteousness, and fulfill their unique calling in Christ.

We need more of these families. There can't ever be too many of such families. There is a dearth of these families today. Most of you will get just one chance to create such a family. Please, choose wisely. We need you to make a wise choice.

Notes

Chapter 2: The Great Exception

1. Debra Lieberman and Elaine Hatfield, "Passionate Love: Cross-Cultural and Evolutionary Perspectives," in *The New Psychology of Love*, ed. Robert Sternberg and Karin Weis (New Haven, CT: Yale University Press, 2006), 280.

2. Vinita Mehta, "The Allure of Aggressive Men," *Psychology Today*, May 28, 2013, www.psychologytoday.com/us/blog/head-games/201305/the-allure-aggressive-men.

Chapter 3: Infatuated with Infatuation

1. Helen Fisher, "The Drive to Love," in *The New Psychology of Love*, ed. Robert Sternberg and Karin Weis (New Haven, CT: Yale University Press, 2006), 88.

2. Fisher, "The Drive to Love," 88.

3. Thomas Lewis, "Twenty-First Century Love: The Neurological Underpinnings of Human Relationships," *San Francisco Medicine* 82, no. 6 (July/August 2009): 13, http://issuu.com/sfmedsociety/docs/july-august.

4. Cited in Kelly Dickerson, "Love's effect on the brain is as powerful as heroin or cocaine" Oct. 12, 2015, www.businessinsider.com/loves-effect-on-the-brain-is-as-powerful-as-heroin-2015-10

5. Helen Fisher, Arthur Aron, and Lucy L. Brown, "Romantic Love: A Mammalian Brain System for Mate Choice," *Philosophical Transactions of the Royal Society* 361 no. 1476 (November 2006): 2173–186, https://royalsocietypublishing.org/doi/10.1098/rstb.2006.1938.

6. David M. Buss, "The Evolution of Love in Humans," in Sternberg and Weis, *The New Psychology of Love*, 76.

7. Buss, "The Evolution of Love," 76.

8. Buss, "The Evolution of Love," 80.

9. Buss, "The Evolution of Love," 77–79.

10. Paul Friesen, *Before You Save the Date: 21 Questions to Help You Marry with Confidence* (Bedford, MA: Home Improvement Ministries, 2010), 53.

11. Fisher, "The Drive to Love," 91–92.

Chapter 4: You May Not Want What You Think You Want

1. Kayt Sukel, *Dirty Minds: How Our Brains Influence Love, Sex, and Relationships* (New York: Free Press, 2012), ebook, loc. 3583.

2. Sukel, Dirty Minds, loc. 3588.

3. *Titanic*, directed by James Cameron (Los Angeles: Twentieth Century Fox, 1997).

Chapter 5: Soul Mate or Sole Mate?

1. *Jerry Maguire*, directed by Cameron Crowe (Los Angeles: TriStar Pictures, 1996).

2. "The State of Our Unions 2001," The National Marriage Project, Rutgers University, June 2001, www.stateofourunions.org/pdfs/SOOU2001.pdf.

3. Plato, *Symposium*, translated by Seth Benardete (Chicago: University of Chicago Press, 1993), 19.

4. Plato, *Symposium*, 20.

5. Plato, *Symposium*, 20.

Chapter 6: A Match Made in Heaven?

1. I'm drawing here on the expositional insight of Dr. Bruce Waltke, *Genesis: A Commentary* (Grand Rapids, MI: Zondervan, 2001), 328.

Chapter 8: Better to Marry Than Burn

1. Deborah Lieberman and Elaine Hatfield, "Passionate Love : Cross-Cultural and Evolutionary Perspectives," in *The New Psychology of Love*, ed. Robert Sternberg and Karin Weis (New Haven, CT: Yale University Press, 2006), 277.

2. Paul Yelsma and Kuriakose Athappilly, "Marital Satisfaction and Communication Practices: Comparisons among Indian and American Couples," *Journal of Comparative Family Studies* 19. no. 1 (Spring 1988): 37–54.

Chapter 9: What's Your Style?

1. Most of these titles are taken from a table in Robert Sternberg, "A Duplex Theory of Love," *The New Psychology of Love*, ed. Robert Sternberg and Karin Weis (New Haven: Yale University Press, 2006), 192. But I've added some and altered the meaning and wording of others for my own purposes.

Chapter 10: Can You Climb a Mountain Together?

1. "Making Screen Magic Is in the Family Script," *USA Today*, June 12, 2011, www.usatoday.com/LIFE/usaedition/2011-06-13-Jada-Pinkett-sidebar_ST_U.htm.

2. Dennis Rainey, *Stepping Up: A Call to Courageous Manhood* (Little Rock, AR: FamilyLife Publishing, 2011), 13–14.

3. Rainey, *Stepping Up*, 14.

Chapter 13: You're Looking for a Complement, Not a Clone

1. Ben Young and Samuel Adams, *The One: A Realistic Guide to Choosing Your Soul Mate* (Nashville: Thomas Nelson, 2001), 92.

Chapter 14: Dating with Intention

1. Janet Brito and Nicole Galan, "Does Sex Provide Health Benefits?" *Medical News Today*, August 23, 2019, www.medicalnewstoday.com/articles/316954?c=664948932756.

Chapter 15: Your Brain on Sex

1. Paul Friesen, *Before You Save the Date: 21 Questions to Help You Marry with Confidence* (Bedford, MA: Home Improvement Ministries, 2010), 129.

2. Friesen, *Before You Save the Date*, 123.

3. Debra Fileta, "Porn Is Not Just a Man's Problem," TrueLoveDates.com, September 20, 2018, https://truelovedates.com/porn-is-not-just-a-mans-problem.

4. Fileta, "Porn Is Not Just a Man's Problem."

Chapter 17: How Would Jesus Date?

1. R. Somerset Ward, *To Jerusalem: Devotional Studies in Mystical Religion* (Harrisburg, PA: Morehouse, 1984), 91.

2. Ward, 91–92.

3. Ward, 92.

4. Ward, 94.

5. Ward, 94.

Chapter 18: Knowing When It's No

1. Ben Young and Samuel Adams, *The One* (Nashville: Thomas Nelson, 2001), 150–51.

2. Byron and Carla Weathersbee, *Before Forever: How Do You Know That You Know?* (Waco, TX: Leading Edge, 2008), 27–29. Used by permission.

3. Weathersbee, 38–39.

Epilogue: A New Vision

1. Robert J. Morgan, *On This Day: 365 Amazing and Inspiring Stories about Saints, Martyrs and Heroes* (Nashville: Thomas Nelson, 1997), February 15.

2. Gary Thomas, *Sacred Marriage* (Nashville: Thomas Nelson, 2000), 268.

Author Information

You can contact and/or follow Gary through the following:

Twitter: @garyLthomas
Facebook: www.facebook.com/authorgarythomas
Instagram: garythomasbooks

Gary writes two blogs, both of which can be found on his website: www.garythomas.com.
One blog is called *Closer to Others* and addresses singles and married people; the other is called *Closer to Christ* and addresses spiritual growth.

For information about having Gary speak at your church, please visit his website: www.garythomas.com/contact.

Please understand that while Gary enjoys reading your feedback, he isn't a licensed counselor and it's not appropriate for him to try to conduct counseling via email.